THE LISTENING HEART

THE
LISTENING
HEART

Vocation and the Crisis of Modern Culture

A. J. CONYERS

SPENCE PUBLISHING COMPANY • DALLAS
2006

Published in the United States by
Spence Publishing Company
111 Cole Street
Dallas, Texas 75207

Library of Congress Control Number: 2006932259

ISBN 1-890626-68-6
978-1-890626-68-6

Printed in the United States of America

To the faculty, the founders,
the students, the staff, and the alumni
of the George W. Truett Theological Seminary

and to

Pastor Naasson Hitimana of Rwanda
and the Christian Cultural Awareness
and Assistance League (C-CAAL)

Contents

The Nomadic Generation
and Its Obstinate Dissenters

When things are displaced, they are always on the move
until they come to rest where they are meant to be.

St. Augustine, *Confessions* 13.9

THIS BOOK IS WRITTEN FOR THOSE who cannot, for their life, take modern western culture at face value. A culture survives and flourishes to the extent that its values are taken to be natural and self-evident. Yet I know there are those who question: who saw in the 1960s not a liberating new epoch, but the working-out of a certain decadence that had been predicted for many years, even centuries. These dissidents of the modern spirit see in the fashions and moral irresponsibility, in the cult of self-destruction among the young and the selfish flight of the old from family responsibilities; in the flagrant violations of ancient taboos in everyday speech; in the loss of courting and romance, frequently now reduced to animal coupling without ceremony, promise, or rite; and in the unwillingness to say that even the most perverse forms of sexual behavior should be censured, the shape of a culture that is dying. They see in the fleeting evanescence of a society with obscene wealth, projections cast upon the dark screens of surfeited and jaded souls. And they see in this culture the marketing of public depravity among the many for the sake of the private wealth of the few.

This book is written for those who suspect that this modern, western world, even with its wealth and its productivity, lacks something essential to the human spirit. They see with their own eyes the army of "homeless" in the cities and along the highways in a land of unimagined wealth. At the same time, they sense an even deeper displacement that is more than geographic and deeper than material poverty, though it is a related phenomenon. There are, as it were, refugees of the spirit in a wealthy but spiritually impoverished part of the world. Too many people are refugees in their own land, some outwardly wandering from place to place, some inwardly. They are displaced people, wanderers who do not really know what to call home. What is often referred to as "home" is merely a convenient place to rest between days of work. The majority of the people they work with, and too often even the ones they live with, are little more than strangers. Deep abiding relationships are not altogether missing in this world, but they are all too rare. Acquaintances are referred to as friends; strangers are called by their first name; but friendship and even the kind of kinship that was built on long years of life together, mutual trust, and sympathetic spirit, are so rare in some places that they seem to be altogether missing from common public conversation. The experience of community is one that is much discussed because there is a deep hunger for it; but it is this very thing that is so elusive.

Peer groups, so-called, or really age groups, become more significant than family in the socializing of the young and increasingly in the social life of middle-aged and of the elderly. A market oriented society, of course, finds this more commodious. Families naturally impose a hierarchy of moral judgments, based upon the interdependency of generations and the availability of experience. Markets often find this inconvenient. Families are frustratingly resistant to the persuasions of commerce; but generation-x, for instance, has no set character and represents, furthermore, great masses of buyers and clients. And then one does not really belong to a "generation" the way one belongs to a family, a church, or a city. The generation has a statistical reality, but not a flesh and blood one. The fact that the category "teenager" began in the early twentieth century is significant. For this marked a transition in which those who formerly would have been considered either dependent children, or young adults with adult responsibility, could be statistically designated as a population with only one real function in the economy: that of emerging customers. They are no longer so attached to families that their purchases are decided by others, nor yet adults with responsibility for earning as well as buying. The more these statistical groups could understand themselves as independent of the family, and from other generations in a community, the better it was for business—especially for some businesses, notably entertainment which experienced enormous growth, and the clothing industry which could produce what amounted to a series of fashion uniforms for the young, all the while convincing the young through ubiquitous advertising that they were declaring their independence!

At the same time, important decisions in society were being made in remote, or at least highly inaccessible places like Washington and London. The growth of bureaucracies in capital cities and the remoteness of the centers of power increased the feeling of alienation from those who make truly adult decisions in society. Absentee authorities more and more governed the common course of life, leaving the ordinary citizen with a sense of impotence in a world barren of meaningful social groups. Social bodies with influence were now less like families and more like armies. It is no accident that the twentieth century world began to evolve from a patchwork of distinct cultural communities to that of very similar armed camps. All the while, wars were never as frequent, nor as ruinous, nor as totally demanding. From its rhetoric, one would think that the modern state is about peace; but from its actions, one can be certain it is organized for war.

This book, therefore, attempts to answer some basic questions for those who would like to know if their senses have failed them, or if, in fact, something significant is palpably missing from life in the midst of such a world. Walker Percy once spoke of the plethora of life-affirming books in our culture; and where there is such a flood of materials affirming life, one can be sure there is a lot of death around. Is there a reason for this widely shared sense of alienation? Are there concepts that help us to understand what is missing and what needs to be recovered? Is there a model for life that would help the recovery of real fellowship, of genuine life together? Can it be that the church is such a model when she has not, herself, succumbed to the prevailing anti-culture of late modernity?

Is there a reason that the community with the most far-reaching common vision, an ecumenical vision, began with a Man who claimed nothing for himself, but answered to a call that ultimately meant his death?

The chapters ahead trace the meaning of the religious experience of vocation, in terms of a Christian theology of vocation. Here we find an alternative to the centrality of "choice." For it is precisely "choice," when it is the first word in our ethical vocabulary, that pulls us apart, and likewise "vocation" that calls us together. These concepts take more time to develop. But in them we find, I believe, the centrifugal forces that pull us apart and make inevitable this sense of alienation of which I have spoken; and also the gravitational center which calls us together and restores the meaning of community, fellowship, and a meaningful, responsible life together.

I am tempted to say that this is a theology of vocation and a sociology of the community. But I am reluctant to say this because I would be misunderstood on both counts. Theology is nowadays often understood as an intellectual exercise concerning God and related subjects that, even if it is done in the church, is actually detachable from the church without much loss either to theology or the church. Sociology is understood as the study of society through the use of empirical methods of discovering its "laws." This is neither. Instead, I take theology to mean discourse about God for the sake of life in community; and I take sociology to mean discourse about society for the sake of life with God. They are two ends of the same subject matter. What one believes about God shapes the way one lives with others in community. And what one knows of society, if you indeed believe in God, cannot be complete if it does not take into consideration the enormous fact of God.

There are, I suppose, a number of things that make up the immediate background of my interest in the questions posed here. My own students, seminary students at the George W. Truett Theological Seminary, are faced with questions of why the church, which should embody a community of peace is often caught up in conflict and division. Such was always the case, of course; but in this context we face the divisions within the fellowship of the Southern Baptist Convention, a conflict that dates back to about 1979, and would probably not have happened except in the midst of an affluent society where the careers of clergy have come to be shaped more by the lure of office and avarice than by vocation and sacrifice. These young people are perhaps more aware than most that neither side has acquitted itself admirably or with much integrity. The seminary's attempt to distance itself from petty denominational strife was only partly successful.

Into the midst of this came a student who had just escaped the horrors of civil war in Rwanda. Phoebe Nyiraneza (now Wabara) knew the failures of the church in her own country, especially when its representatives actually collaborated with the killings. But she also saw courage in the church—especially that of her own father, a president of the Rwandan Presbyterian Church, who stood off a mob at his front door and would not deliver into their hands the victims they sought. He did that even though he was a Hutu and his guests were Tutsi. She also saw that kind of dedication in a number of young Christians who gave their own lives rather than give in to the demonic forces of the mob.

This large and deadly conflict is palely reflected in the petty conflicts of a more domestic kind, the kind one observes even in the church. Conflicts both large and small raise the questions, "What are the sources of community?" and "What lies behind our wars and fightings at every level?" These are the kinds of questions I hope to explore in this book.

I wish to dedicate these efforts to those who, by their heroic lives, have helped me to understand the issues involved in community, in a longing for peace with justice, and in the price required to witness to the truth of our times, unhinged as they are from the principles that make for peace. These are the true dissidents. Those of my heroes are too numerous to list, though their number is miniscule beside the population that suffers so pitiably at the hands of the power-hungry, the greedy, and those with hearts full of violence and hate in today's world. One will represent them all. He is mentioned above: Pastor Hitimana, a Rwandan Presbyterian pastor, whose faithful witness brought solace and hope to many in the midst of the bloody war in Rwanda in 1994. It is also dedicated to my friends in Christian Cultural Awareness and Assistance League (C-CAAL), an organization founded by Christian and Phoebe Wabara and made up of men and women from every continent and every race on earth for the purpose of helping those whose communities have been destroyed by war and informing those whose communities are undermined by secularism. Finally it is dedicated to my students who wish to understand the gospel of peace in a world that, both near and far, rings loud with the tocsins of war.

THE LISTENING HEART

The Era of Bloodshed

What causes wars, and what causes fightings among you?

THIS QUESTION, posed by the Apostle James, hangs suspended above the dark side of our world, today as in his day. It is the lesser light of our existence, and in dark times it does not so much shed light as remind us of a certain lunacy in the human make-up. Why in this modern world have humane communities—communities that for brief moments in history rise above strife and in fact nourish the human spirit, enrich the mind, provide for the safety and education of the young—proven so hard to come by, so difficult to maintain, and known it seems only to our most nostalgic moments? Why have the "wars and fightings" of this past century taken more lives, destroyed more communities, exiled more people, decimated more ethnic groups than ever before in any comparable time? Why have more people been killed by their own governments in this past century than in all other times together? How is it that this new century has gotten off to such an unpromising start? James had an answer that tapped into the root of human nature, and into the human lunacy:

"Is it not your passions that are at war in your members? You desire and do not have; so you kill. And you covet and cannot obtain; so you fight and wage war."[1]

This book might be considered a commentary on that one question and its answer, and on the hope which frames this question. In the church, the Apostle saw the promise of another kind of community, one that is "first pure, then peaceable, gentle, open to reason, full of mercy and good fruits" and in which "the harvest of righteousness is sown in peace by those who make peace." What is the difference between these kinds of communities? Is one merely reality and the other a vain wish? Or do the roots that nourish each community lie deep inside the human experience of those who, in different ways, have learned to hope or to fear: whether out of generosity and justice they have learned to trust each other and to trust existence itself; or whether out of competing desires they have learned to fear each other and distrust the world into which they are born. The philosopher of the modern age, Thomas Hobbes, claimed that the beginning of wisdom is to know that "each is at war with each"; on that note, the modern world emerged. Though it would more often than not paint its philosophy with a kindlier face than Hobbes did, modernity still believed the world was made bearable only by power and wealth, not justice and generosity.

Violence and the decline of community

Sooner or later violence overtakes a society that functions chiefly on the basis of the rivalry of competitive desires, on the basis of choice, or on the basis of "freedom" defined as the unhindered will. Modern secular society is the longest experiment in history attempting to elevate "choice" or this kind of freedom to the level of a basic social principle. It should not be surprising, though I think to many the awareness of this has not surfaced, that modern life is also the most violent period in the history of mankind. Recent events fill us with foreboding, but also with a new awareness of how close is the connection between egocentric desires and the outbreak of violence. For where desire must first be satisfied, whether on the personal or the national level, before the virtues of a just, patient, and generous life are attended to, then conflict (always with us in any event) finds no mediating principle to which it might appeal, no reason for forbearance, and no hope for resolution.

What gives these passions the occasion, however, to be transformed into bloodshed? The twentieth century, an age that was prodigal of all kinds of violence, produced three important theories about the sources of violent behavior on a wide scale in society. First, Hannah Arendt suggested that where power, in the sense of effective action within a community is missing, violence takes its place. Moreover, once the institutions of government have outgrown the individual and the neighborhood, so that the very scale of governance no longer permits effective action for most people, then those people are more likely to take to the streets and address their grievances in destructive ways. Second, René Girard claims that violence gives focus and directs our competing desires in such a way that community is strengthened by a mutual turning against a scapegoat or an enemy. Thus the collective shape of society, its very possibility for community, feeds off a fundamental injustice and attachments to common hatreds. Moreover, in Girard's view, modern society, long tutored by the Christian gospel in the awareness of injustice and the innocence of its victims, finds itself in a crisis of contradiction precisely over the issue of violence and peace. Third, Eric Voegelin taught that once society becomes closed to those experiences by which it is shaped, namely its reach for transcendent meaning, and the human quest focuses instead on worldly goods, the competing demands are satisfied by nothing short of bloodshed and revolution. All three of these views overlap at a critical point: human beings naturally reach for meaningful action, and not finding it, resort to irrational and destructive action. All of these theories begin, as we can easily see, with what James has called "the passions . . . at war in your members." All of these theories, I believe, are important for understanding the kinds of conditions that give rise to violence and the uses to which violence is traditionally given over. It is no wonder, of course, that the twentieth century has made possible some of history's profoundest reflections on the sources of violence.

"Vocation" or "choice"?

This book turns the question in a different direction. It asks instead about the shape of social forces influenced by something other than egocentric desires, competing ambitions, autonomous freedom, or the freedom to choose. A contrary motivation—more common in history than we often realize—is expressed in the idea of "vocation." More than an idea, in fact, one might say that it is a certain orientation of life, a strong sentiment that is essential to the building of a humane community. In every society that is essentially humane in its ideal expression, some element of "vocation" dwells at the heart of its self-understanding.

Of course the obverse side of that question also comes into view: What happens when a society loses this idea of its existence and of what shapes its existence? The sentiment of "being called," of experiencing life as a pilgrimage, is not, of course, altogether missing from modern life, but it is a much diminished idea without the attractive and compelling presence that it once had. It has been reduced to philosophies about "work" or "occupation," or confined to the church "professions." Rightly understood, however, it is a view in which human life is drawn toward some purpose that is greater than the individual, one that stands above national interests, that invests life with nobility and beauty, and that creates "room" for the common life. More than "work" and more than a "religious identity" or membership in a religious community, it is the notion that being human means one is drawn toward a destiny—and not simply as a worker or as a religionist, but as a soul that properly belongs to that which is yet dimly seen, but which already lays claim to one's very existence.

Vocation and community

Senator Sam Ervin told the story of a rural Baptist congregation near Murphy, North Carolina, that had decided to sell its property and move to another location. The church found a buyer and was about to close the transaction when a search for the deed revealed that the church fathers, in the pioneer days of that mountain community, had deeded the property to "the Lord God Almighty." Not knowing how to proceed, the realtor went to a lawyer to find out how close the sale. Taking a few days to think it over, the lawyer ran into a judge on the streets of Murphy and told him about the church's dilemma. "What would you do?" he asked. The old judge replied, "It's very simple. You run an announcement in the paper, requesting the stated owner to make it known if he still has any interest in the property and that, absent any objection from said owner, the property will be disposed of by the deacons of the church. Then, after a couple of weeks, you run another announcement to this effect: "After thorough and diligent search, the Lord God Almighty cannot be found in Cherokee County, North Carolina—and therefore legal standing for the disposition of property will be transferred to the deacons of the church.'"

If this story has a comic twist to contemporary ears, it also has a note of tragedy. Both the comedy and the tragedy hinge upon a gradual but very definite loss of the kind of sentiment that made it possible, once, for rural land owners, well beyond the eastern fringes of civilization, to file a deed of ownership to "the Lord God Almighty." We laugh not so much for what they had, but for what we no longer have, a sense of entering into a transaction with the Almighty—a covenant of sorts. It was no doubt meant to be irrevocable: that piece of land, that sacred alter, that graveyard of beloved parents and children, as permanent as anything can be in a world that inevitably changes. And those who signed their names to such a document would doubtless have had as much trouble imagining our secular prejudices against such transactions as we do their simple faith.

While they may not have considered what confusion would ensue in a society where buying and selling became frenetic, where the mode of social life had reverted to the nomadic, and where transactions had fallen into the hands of those expert at legal pettifoggery, they did assume other things that, even at first glance, don't seem unreasonable. They assumed that the aim of settlement was to achieve as much permanence as possible and that transactions were more personal covenants protected by a sense of honor, than documents crafted by lawyers to trap men in a net of words.

Moreover, they lived in a world where certain words and certain stories carried enormous weight. I have a photograph taken by a New York photographer only about seventy-five years ago.[2] It is the image of a Baptist preacher from that same community. He looks with piercing eyes, out of a semi-emaciated visage, into the camera. His gaze is harmless, even kind, and yet the sense of dignity in the man is conveyed even over the years and the changes that stand between us. From the eyes of the man, one's attention is immediately drawn to the enormous book that he holds under his left arm—a Bible, every bit as large as a pulpit text, or one of those family Bibles that are still sold, but not nearly in the quantity that they once were. These words that he clutched to his side were "God's words." He was a messenger of those words. Unlike the lawyer's words, they were not intended to secure all things in a surface netting, but to cut deep into reality and into human minds and hearts. These words lead further into mystery; the words of the lawyer are intended to expel mystery.

My intention in recalling this image, and these stories, is not to engage in a bit of nostalgia, or to suggest in any way that an era, or a people now remote from our experience, were not plagued by the same kinds of serious problems that we face, and some that we do not. But memories, even memories that come to us through photographs and anecdotes, have a way of provoking us to take stock of a resource we might have neglected. These people were very much more conscious, I would venture to say, of life as an encounter between the divine and the human—one in which the issues of life are decided on the basis of a divine call and a human response. If such a view of life was at all true then, it is no less true today; and the advantages of recognizing that fact are as needed now as then. The intention of this book is to explore the possibility that the loss of community, about which we hear almost daily laments from observers of the modern scene, is related to the loss of a sense of vocation. I want to suggest, in different ways, that the conviction of a divine calling draws from us the kinds of commitment, the level of patience, and the degree of hope that makes community life possible. It is this conviction that made the West a place of humane dwelling—if ever there was such a place—and it is the corruption and loss of this conviction that partly explains our present crisis.

First we must examine what it means for a well disposed community to exist with a certain conviction about vocation, and what it means when the community is no longer under the spell of "choice."

2

Vocation and Community

*Here we have the very heart of the earthly city. Its God (or
gods) is he or they who will help the city to victory after
victory and to a reign of earthly peace; and this city worships,
not because it has any love for service, but because its passion
is for domination. This, in fact, is the difference between good
and bad men, that the former make use of the world in order
to enjoy God, whereas the latter would like to make use of
God in order to enjoy the world—if, of course, they believe in
God and his providence over man . . .*

Augustine, *The City of God*

THE IDEA OF "VOCATION"—of being "called"—is at first commonplace until one actually begins to think what an extraordinary thing is suggested by such language. It suggests, of course, that life does not center on the choices of individuals, and that community does not emerge entirely by appealing to those choices the way modern societies ever since the industrial age assumed, being wholly distracted by the wealth-making power of the market and its appeal to the individual consumer. Vocation instead implies that a larger obligation presses itself upon persons and draws them into a community of mutual sacrifice and affection. Not centering in the individual, the obligations and the affections are understood as coming from a transcendent source. Yet while they are not centered in the individual, they are necessarily addressed to the individual, and therefore necessarily personal—and if personal they can only be described as coming from a divine source, from God. It is that extraordinary premise of community life that the modern age, like the builders of the tower at Babel, wished to defy, even if it could not altogether deny it.

A condition strongly implied in the Christian view of life, it is even to be found in non-Christian religious sentiment. Indeed, without this strong predisposition to think that people are moved by a "calling" that originates above and beyond them, rather than acting on the basis of a personal "choice" that is easily revoked, a community that has a sense of its own permanence and can invest in improving quality of life and in real cultural achievements is not possible.

Yet in modern Western culture, while there are vestiges of the original sentiment in the language, the actual idea of "vocation" is strangely missing or misunderstood. Almost as soon as it was broadened and made prominent in Protestant theologies of the sixteenth century, its sense began to be lost, or at least to become secularized. It is my belief that many of the disorders that we associate with modern life—the social alienation, the breakdown of so-called mediating institutions such as the family, the violence that so marked the last century that it must, ahead of all else, be known as the most violent century—are tied to the loss of a sentiment of "vocation." And something of this sort must be realized before culture takes on the character of a humane culture, giving rise to communities where people actually thrive and prosper in a sense not purely material. This is the true burden of this essay, to reconstruct in the mind of a careful and considerate reader what it means to live in a society dominated by vocation, rather than one dominated by the will and the notion of "choice."

To put this another way, societies, and human relationships and actions in general, are dominated either by the strength of a certain attraction—attraction to one another, to the beauty of what is made, to the justice of what is done—or by the will and the power and the "choice" that is invested in another. The actions and relationships of men and women are determined by love, or they are determined by force. As Henri Bergson once showed, both are in play at once.[1] But it is important to know that these things are enhanced to the extent that they come by love, and they are diminished to the extent they are enforced through the imposition of another's will. The Church is an institution whose authority derives most essentially from its invocation of divine love and its power to engender human love. The modern age, however, founded just as the waning ecumenical powers of the Church reached their lowest point, based itself upon power—power in the new nation states, power in its economic organization of things, power in the new idea of science as that through which men became "the masters and possessors of nature." Now that the limits of modernity have become apparent to almost everyone, now that modernity has lost that "self-evident" justification it once possessed, and now that people are willing to think in terms of "post-modernity," the question is open once more, "Shall we heal a broken society through love, or through power?"

Towards a definition

The familiar term "vocation," used in both religious and secular contexts, is rooted in the Latin *vocatio*, meaning "call" and is related to Latin-based words such as "voice" and "invoke." The Greek word is *klesis* and is found in our words "cleric," and "ecclesiastical." It is the root of the New Testament word for the Church, *ekklesia*, a point that is not etymologically significant except in that assemblies of all kinds were referred to with the same term. To say that the church consists of those "called out," however, is significant for more reasons than can be traced through linguistic usage: it was the reality to which the church had always attested.

In both Judeo-Christian and in non-Judaic contexts, the human sentiment of a divine call plays an important role, and gives to the society in which it is embedded a certain character that we would find to be distinctly non-modern. Here are a few points that highlight the distinction.

First, the idea of a call implies an agent outside of the one who is subject to the call. One does not simply "choose" a course of action, but one responds to a summons. A person might be "free" in either case; but in the case of one responding to vocation, the freedom is not an inner-directed impulse, but the use of the will to respond to an unforeseen and perhaps unknown reality. This summons is characteristic of various reports, in a great variety of communities, from the summons of Zarathustra (the Iranian Zoroaster), to the calling forth of Abraham and the divine election of Moses, to the call of Isaiah, the baptism of Jesus, the blinding of Paul, the spiritual apparitions of Joan of Arc, and the divine compulsions of Martin Luther. The character in each case is founded on the summons that is *external* to the one who is called. Here, and in the following points about the nature of vocation, I am not particularly interested in either establishing or refuting the validity of the experiences as in showing something of the character of the experience: for here I simply wish to distinguish between a society that incorporates a sentiment of vocation and one that explains its behavior in other ways.

Second, the summons is often *against* the will of the one who is called into service. Muhammed first believed himself to be mad. Moses complained that the Israelites, to whom God sent him, had never listened to him and therefore neither would Pharaoh, "poor speaker that I am."[2] Jeremiah, the Hebrew prophet, not only resisted the call, but continued to complain that God had overpowered him and placed him in an impossibly difficult circumstance, even protesting that God's call had made him "like a gentle lamb led to the slaughter."[3] Jonah attempted to flee from the Lord to Tarshish, rather than going to Ninevah where he had been called. Jesus prayed to be delivered from his appointed calling.

It is often noted that Enlightenment thinkers emphasized reason. Yet the real effect of their emphasis is almost always lost. This certainly could not mean that they emphasized reason while earlier ages neglected it, or preferred superstition and unreason: who indeed were more devoted to the arts of reason than the disciples of Aristotle in antiquity, or those who, in medieval times, submitted everything to reason in the most rigorous fashion, the schoolmen from Anselm to Aquinas and beyond? The specific way in which the Enlightenment used reason was *as a replacement for the idea of vocation*. One could then make *reasoned choices*. The true locus of personal decisions was to be found in the individual who "thinks for himself," as Kant would put it, and who declines to depend upon the "guidance of another." That reason does not have to be thought of in this individualistic way is shown by Gerhart Niemeyer when he said that the "creators of philosophy never spoke of reason in the way Enlightenment thinkers did." In fact, what they said was closer to the idea of vocation:

> Parminides experienced the Is in a vision; Socrates, Plato, and others experienced being "drawn," "pulled," even "dragged" to the true reality beyond the cosmos. They respond to these experiences with something they call "the quest," "the arduous way," "the search," clearly conveying that the authority of truth is not found in themselves, nor in their method, but in their participation in a higher reality. Their attitude was one of love of the cosmos and of divine wisdom. Where in the Enlightenment do we find mention of "love" to characterize the attitude towards the cosmos or divinity? Enlightenment focuses on the objects of

knowledge which mind can convert from multiplicity to unity, or from unity to composing parts, all for the sake of human control and mastery over nature.[4]

Third, the calling involves in almost every case hardships that must be overcome in order to answer the summons. Jeremiah, Ezekiel, Muhammed, Mani (the founder of Manichaeism), Socrates, Jesus, and Paul all found themselves under threat of death by their community. Zarathustra is sent into exile. Jesus' moment of public vocation is followed by temptation in the wilderness. Paul's vocation is accompanied by physical ailments, imprisonment, beatings, and exile.

Fourth, from the point of view of answering to the summons, the greatest danger appears not in this kind of resistance, but in the possibility of being *diverted* or *distracted* from the goal. The whole of Joshua's reiteration of the covenant with Israel, after they had settled the land of Canaan, was devoted to the threat and the consequences of being distracted from their promise to "serve the Lord" and to the warning against being tempted by other gods. In all of the Deuteronomic history of Israel—that history contained in the books of Joshua, Judges, Samuel, and Kings—the chief standard by which the nations of Israel and Judah and their kings are judged is their faithfulness to God, measured by their resistance to distraction by the religions of their neighbors. And the last petition in Jesus' model prayer, "lead us not into temptation, but deliver us from evil," is an invocation against this distraction.

These distinctive features of vocation found in traditional societies help us to mark off what is now different in our own modern and Western culture. While the sentiment is still there in form and in vocabulary, its striking force and its assault upon the ego are all but dissolved.

I was involved, at my university, in a project funded by Lilly Endowment, Incorporated, for the design and implementation of programs for students and others associated with universities on the idea of vocation. Our preparation required a considerable amount of time devoted to research into the theory of vocation. As I surveyed the literature in this field, I was struck by the fact that most modern books about vocation were actually about "work." In most cases the initial implication of the word "call" was quickly passed over in order to make the next connection, the one with which most modern readers are familiar since the word itself has come to mean little more than "occupation," the way one makes a living.

Protestants generally remember to congratulate themselves on the heritage of making vocation broader than the "monastic" calling, but then are just as inattentive to the fact that the word has a broader meaning than the work and the offices (secular and religious) that a person might fill. There is no reason, for instance, that a person might not be called to *leave* a work. The biblical picture of the "call" is quite as likely to entail someone leaving their work as it is to taking up work, and twice as likely to involve leaving as it is to taking up respectable public employment. After all, Matthew left his tax collecting, John, James, Peter, and Andrew left their fishing business, Moses left his desert sheep tending, Jeremiah left the priesthood, and Amos left his sycamore dressing—all in response to a call. So the contemporary literature we found, even some of the best of it, concentrates upon the secondary rather than the primary meaning of vocation.

The attenuated nature of many of these treatments became especially apparent as we stood them end to end against some of the early great figures in Christian thought who commented upon vocation with a strong emphasis upon this primary idea of a person or community responding to a "call' from God. In these works—and I am thinking particularly of Origen, Athanasius and Augustine—the idea of vocation, of being "called" is a rich and powerful idea. Really, one should say that it goes beyond the "idea." It is something evocative of an experience of being drawn, pulled, tugged, newly fashioned, almost if not completely killed, for the sake of that which calls you on. It has to do with the whole person, body and soul, transported in a way that is at once profoundly disordering and profoundly ordering. It is the word that means, at once, death and life, the loss of freedom and the discovery of freedom in a new way, setting one at once against the community to which you are born, and yet done so for the sake of that community. The Church Fathers recognized that such a sense of "calling" was the very essence of the Church. For to be called to follow Christ was to be called to die on a cross: the fellowship of the church was the communion of those who had, in a profound sense, accepted the sentence of death in order to transcend it in a new life.

It is important to note that this word "call" is an experience, or speaks of an experience, that runs in the opposite direction from the social experience most often articulated by modern people. Here is an idea that pictures the self being "laid hold of" by another, having a claim made upon his time, his future, his destiny, the shape of his life that originates from outside the self. It is the opposite of "choice," or of freedom in the sense of self-determination.

I was struck with how far we had lost sight of the sentiment embedded in "vocation" when I ran across the title of a mid-twentieth century book that was given as "How to Choose Your Vocation"! Precisely the point of *vocatio* is that you *don't* choose. And this is precisely why and how the idea jars against conventional modern sentiment, the sentiment that since the Enlightenment has succeeded in making a primary virtue of self-determination. "What is Enlightenment?" asked Immanuel Kant. It is the capacity "to use one's intelligence without being guided by another." "Have courage to use your own intelligence! is therefore the motto of the enlightenment."[5] Thus stand side by side, in unmistakable opposition, two ideas of the way one lives in the world. One is that of attentive listening to the guidance of another, whether of a wise guide, or tradition, or of God. The other is the notion of the self-determined "free" man, who without listening to another, becomes the master of his own soul.

It is not without significance that Kant, like others following the same pattern, appeals to a virtue of the will, courage. For in many ways the movement of modernity has been a shift from the intellect and the affections as guiding faculties for human beings, to the will. Kants does not say, develop the skill to think for yourself. Nor does he say learn what best to love so that you may guide yourself toward what is good. Nor does he suggest that you have the courage to follow what you know is good and true. The will is placed ahead of the intellect and the love of good. He says instead, "All that is required for enlightenment is *freedom*. . . ."[6] and "Men raise themselves by and by out of backwardness if one does not purposely invent artifices to keep them down."[7]

Over against this is the understanding of life that has always struck human beings as belonging to the province of common sense. We came into a world that existed before us. We leave this world long before things resolve themselves in a way that gives moral or intellectual clarity to the situation in which we find ourselves. So, in order to live here with any semblance of wisdom, purpose, and order, we need "the guidance of another." We "think for ourselves" only in the most narrow and limited sense. In most cases we depend heavily upon the traditions and the common prejudices of our civilization. And the religious insight is that these traditions and prejudices are capable of being kept on track because of the reality of special revelatory occasions. These occasions, the oracle of a prophecy, the mighty acts of God in specific historical events, the miracles or teachings of one specially sent by God, become a part of the common possessions of mankind that offer insights into the truth of things. While their source is something or someone quite rare that constitutes a peculiarity within the human experience, their applications are corporate and even universal.

In fields highly dependent upon technology, the corporate nature of knowledge is so apparent that we all take it for granted. None of us drives an automobile—or at least very few of us—and think we understand all that goes into the running of it. We are dependent upon a whole host of engineers, chemists, physicists, technicians, metallurgists, artists, glaziers, who seldom even understand each other, but whose collective labors make a car and enable someone like me to drive it. Yet the modern prejudice (in the negative sense of an unexamined mistake) is that in the higher matters of morals, philosophy, religion, and politics, we need no one but ourselves.

This distinctly modern prejudice might be called the "Invictus" principle. We think for ourselves; we are the masters of our souls. In more ancient texts, such as the Old Testament book of Judges, such a characteristic in society was thought to be the sign of profound disorder rather than a sign of freedom. The woeful story of idolatry and violence in the last chapters of that book is punctuated with the lament that "in those days there was no king in Israel; every man did what was right in his own eyes."[8] This disorder furthermore was the essence of a violent life, and an unrelentingly murderous way of life. It is not without profound significance, I think, that the one who was executed for the worst crime of domestic terrorism in United States history used as his final statement a hand-written copy of William Ernest Henley's "Invictus." The poem ends with the lines "I am the master of my fate;/I am the captain of my soul."

Vocation in the Christian theological tradition

Christian theology of a divine calling, or vocation, begins with the doctrine that springs from the extraordinary disclosure in the first chapter of Genesis that "God created man in his own image."[9] Christians, especially since Origen, have understood this not as a completed act, referring it to the chronological past, nor have they seen it as a simple endowment of humanity with god-like qualities. It was understood as rooted in God's design, but also becoming manifest as a promise. It is dynamic rather than static; something that draws the human being toward God, rather than placing him on his own beside God.

Origen made this point by indicating the two ways in which these words are used in Genesis. First, the text says, "Let us make man in our image, after our likeness."[10] Then, as God fulfills this stated intention, the text says, "So God created man in his own image, in the image of God he created him; male and female he created them."[11] Such was Origen's respect for the very words of Scripture that he believed the omission of "likeness" in the second statement could scarcely have been accidental. It must have been intentional; and it must therefore have meaning.[12] Origen concluded that, while one can say that man is created in the image of God, the image is not yet perfected. That perfection of the *imago* is represented by the word *similitudo*, likeness. As Fr. José Alviar has stated the matter, "The task imposed by God on man upon creating him is, therefore, to become even more like the Maker, enriching and perfecting the original image." Thus the idea of "image" endows human beings with a "fundamental destiny." They experience existence in terms of a tension between what they intuit themselves to be destined for, and what they find themselves to be, between the justice and goodness they are capable of imagining, and where, in that regard, they live.

I was once told, just before going to Taiwan to lead college students in a Bible study, that the Chinese don't comprehend the notion of "sin." Yet when I presented to non-Christian students the idea of sin in these terms, that is in terms of the tension between a certain moral ideal and their satisfaction with their own performance according to that ideal, they understood perfectly well. And this is the very essence of the doctrine of "original sin." We are not faced with the "minimal requirements" of a moral life when we are faced with our sin; nor are we faced with the average or typical behavior of the community. The experience of sin—neither in Christian thought nor in our deepest awareness of reality—is not the experience of a social convention that is imposed upon us. It is rather an awareness of something that "calls" us beyond the experience or the expectations of this life; it is an awareness of being made for something that we have never experienced, and which yet pulls us beyond ourselves. It is the experience, one might say, of vocation. As Fr. Alviar expressed it, in referring to the "labile existence" of the image in which the human being is made: "It is 'already' and at the same time 'not yet' present. In one sense, man possesses the image from the start, as he is rational by essence; in another sense, he possesses the image tenuously, for the achievement of virtue is a contingent process. Man is expected to bring the image to fulfillment, sharing in the Word's attributes not minimally but fully."[13]

The Old Testament concern for the "call of God" generally pertains to the community. Israel is bound to God through its acceptance of a covenant, by which God binds himself irrevocably to the community of Israel. The covenant illuminates the moral dimension of the nation's life. To Abraham, the Lord says, "I am *El Shaddai*; walk before me and be blameless." And the covenant also binds God to this people: "And I will give to you, and to your descendents after you, the land of your sojourning, all the land of Canaan, for an everlasting possession; and I will be their God."[14]

The concern of the Old Testament covenant, and of the Prophets of Israel who proclaim on the basis of that covenant, is clearly tied to the national life of Israel. Even so, as Israel is led into exile, the continued existence of the national life depends in part, at least, on the faithfulness of individuals and families who refuse to be drawn off into the culture of their captivity, first among the Babylonians and later the Persians. Ezekiel's message, while clearly communal in its concern, is addressed, more than was pre-exilic prophecy, to the individual. "O house of Israel," says the god of Ezekiel, "I will judge each of you according to his ways."[15] In this transition from pre-exilic Israelite theology to post-exilic Judaism, we see the rise of the focus on the individual.

A similar movement can be seen in Deuteronomic (prophetic) history, when for example the story is told of Elijah's encounter with the prophets of Baal and its aftermath. Here we see the contrast between, on the one hand, the overpowering public display of an Almighty God, who—as in days of yore—answered with fire, proving his presence in an outward demonstration of his power and, on the other hand, his private answer to Elijah. It is in the cave on Mount Horeb that the true center of the story is found. There it is no longer the God of the parted waters, and the plagues in Egypt, and the consumed alter on Mount Carmel, that is in evidence. Until this point in the narrative, such was always the nature of God's actions among the nations: it was an outward and public display, that was in the most ordinary sense, a communal act—the act of a national God. On Mount Horeb, however, all of the old signs—the great natural powers—are on display. First there is the "great and strong wind," then the earthquake, and finally a fire. But the text reveals that the Lord was not in any of these things. Instead, "after the fire a still small voice." It was in this small voice that only Elijah could hear that the Lord was authentically present.[16]

In the New Testament, an even more remarkable transition takes place. While it is the individual that makes the move toward God, it is no longer also a move toward a covenant nation in an historical sense. Instead, it is toward a new body, a supra-national community. The communal concern here is no longer national, but ecumenical. And it is no longer a legacy from the past, but a promise regarding the future. It retains both a sense of the dignity of the individual and the communal destiny of the individual. Dietrich Bonhoeffer says that at no time is a person more alone than in becoming a Christian, but the alienation is for the sake of a new community.[17] Furthermore, this community transcends the usual divisions. As the Apostle Paul stated it, "There is neither Jew nor Greek, there is neither slave nor free man, there is neither male nor female; for you are all one in Christ Jesus."[18]

There is no doubt that it is to St. Paul that we are most indebted for the richness and the depth of the Christian idea of vocation. He is, as one writer commented, "on several counts . . . destined to remain the most memorable author on the subject."[19] Two features of Paul's writings should strike us in this regard. One is the fact that his language reflects precisely those sentiments that occurred to Gerhart Niemeyer when he was commenting on the broader phenomenon of "reason." The founders of philosophy, Niemeyer said, thought of reason as something that called them to step outside of themselves, and to undergo hardships and dangers, the whole attitude is hardly one of reflecting comfortably from the armchair of the "enlightenment gentleman," based upon superior calculations, but it is the attitude of one engaged in an adventure. The emotional tone conveys that one does not quite know the outcome of such a journey.

Notice in Paul, for instance, his continual reminder to his correspondents of his vocation. I am "Paul, a slave of Jesus Christ, called to be an apostle, set apart for the gospel of God which he promised beforehand through his prophets in the holy scriptures."[20] He writes to those who also are "called to be saints."[21] In the letter to the Romans, this gospel holds him captive, lays obligations upon him, and is a power which compels him. What has been wrought through him has been "by the power of signs and wonders, by the power of the Holy Spirit."[22] To the Corinthians, he describes himself and the other apostles as being "like men sentenced to death," who have become "a spectacle to the world," "fools for Christ's sake," "held in disrepute." Furthermore, he says, "we are ill-clad and buffeted and homeless . . . the refuse of the earth, the off-scouring of all things."[23] For the call of the gospel, he endures "afflictions, hardships, calamities, beatings, imprisonments, tumults, labors, watching, hunger."[24] And in Galatians, he reminds his readers that "I bear on my body the marks of Jesus."[25]

Furthermore, the recognition of this truth of the gospel comes because God "made us alive together with Christ . . . raised us up with him, and made us sit in heavenly places in Christ Jesus." We do not simply "know" the truth in a cognitive sense, but "we are his workmanship."[26]

The other matter of remarkable importance for Paul is the use of the corporate imagery of the "body," the temple, and the household. We find these references throughout the Pauline corpus, and they are similar in concept, whether from Romans 12, 1 Corinthians 12, or Ephesians 2. The idea of "body" is quite dissimilar, and dissimilar in important ways, from the Enlightenment attachment to the organized state. Through liberal democratic ideas, developing out of Hobbes' idea of the state and then taking on their democratic form with the help of English and American thinkers, including John Locke and John Stuart Mill, the most important feature of the "members" of the political "body" came to be equality. Of course, what makes a member of a body significant in the original Pauline metaphor is not its equality but its difference. The hand is different from the eye and so they can each contribute to the unity of the body in their distinct ways. They exist, furthermore, not for themselves but for the sake of the "body." This is an organic concept. The modern idea of the state is, by contrast, the concept of an organization. It is conceived mechanically rather than organically. Equality emphasizes the interchangeability of parts, while the organic body metaphor depends upon the interdependence of the parts. Equality jealously guards the "rights" of individuals, but "membership" in a body emphasizes the contribution to the whole. Liberal democracy values the uniform relationship of the parts to the whole, while the Pauline "body" concept values the eccentric and multiform relationship of the disparate members.

Therefore, the Pauline "vocation" is always to a higher unifying reality, namely the body of Christ. It is, furthermore, an eschatological reality for which one might hope and a reality for which one might long to suffer for its greater glory. "He must increase, but I must decrease" are words appropriate to this sentiment of a greater good calling for the suffering, longing, and diminishing of the person. The Enlightenment state also calls for individual sacrifice, but it does so posing as a deliverer from the petty tyrannies of traditional authorities, such as the church, the tribe, and the family. The irony of this trade-off is apparent, for it profits from diminishing the ties to which the individual is born, or in which the individual abides in common faith, by preaching the enlargement of the individual's sphere of action and privilege. At the same time it requires the kind of sacrifice that is implied in the individual's relationship to family or community of faith.

Since the sixteenth century, the state has become a new kind of community. It is not a true nation, since it is made up generally of many nations, although there is a dominant national culture. Its influence then arises from the fact that it is organized in a way that dissolves what is organic and to some extent voluntary. It should not be surprising then that the concepts of "vocation" and the concept of vocation as it is embedded in the liberal arts has subsided in the public consciousness. Organizations do not need such ideas or experiences, but organic communities do. And it should not be surprising that modernity has been marked by the exaggeration of the freedoms of the individual, the alienation of the person, the dissolution of families, and a culture of pathological loneliness: for these features are in the very design of the organized society which replaces the organic society.

3

The Broken Image

THERE IS NO NEED HERE to rehearse the fact, lamented by various commentators on the doctrine of Christian vocation, that the concept has, by stages, been reduced to the calling to the monastic life, to the life of the priesthood or the religious. Protestants recall Luther's broadening of the idea of vocation to include the work of the laborer and the magistrate, as well as the minister of the church. The lesson was not a new one, but the emphasis was new. Calvin's genius for gaining the balance in a Christian teaching was applied to the idea of vocation as having a double focus, one upon the earthly duty and the other upon the heavenly destiny. In this way the common tasks of the Christian, as well as those more greatly honored in society, are held in new esteem. He writes in the *Institutes* of those tasks as bearing a certain nobility when the person "will bear and swallow the discomforts, vexations, weariness, and anxieties in his way of life, when he has been persuaded that the burden was laid upon him by God." In this way, "no task will be so sordid and base, provided you obey your calling in it, that it will not shine and be reckoned very precious in God's sight."[1]

But the broadening of the concept of vocation was seen by Dietrich Bonhoeffer to have had its own reductionistic effect. Max Weber's definition of vocation as a "limited field of (secular) accomplishment" could be seen as the failure of the Lutheran view to retain vocation as more than "the justification and sanctification of secular institutions."[2] For vocation "in the New Testament sense, is never a sanctioning of worldly institutions as such; its 'yes' to them always includes at the same time an extremely emphatic 'no,' an extremely sharp protest against the world."[3] The monastic system had at least provided the death-defying "no," even if it had failed to adequately provide the life affirming "yes" of Christian vocation. The result of the division in Christendom, however, was seen by Bonhoeffer as having "two disastrous misunderstandings." Both misunderstandings, "the secular Protestant one and the monastic one," were less than the Pauline idea of vocation deserved, and less than the church has at times seen in its fullness.

Behind what is normally seen as an unwarrented reduction of the Christian idea of vocation, however, is a competing idea that is not usually fully appreciated by the biblical scholar and the theologian. The idea of the *imago dei*, with which the early formulation of *vocatio* was so strongly involved, was easily taken in a sense quite different from that expressed by Origen, Augustine, Aquinas, and Luther. These men, fully aware of the eschatological and hopeful dimension of the human character, understood that the image of God in the human being was not a settled fact, but a promise. It was one, to be sure, that shaped the human being and the human community even in the present, but it was nevertheless never to be taken as a source of pride.

To trace a different route for that idea of the image of God is not difficult. The word merely needed to be spoken before there were some who would take it to mean that the human is *endowed* with a god-like character that can be useful in all sorts of ways. Modernity is perhaps a legacy of just such a development. For the medieval period,

especially the Renaissance, is replete with examples of the overween-
ing pride in the human place in the cosmos. Pico della Mirandella is
one who comes readily to mind, with his influential *Oration on the
Dignity of Man*. Frances Yates showed how deftly this most influential
European, this leading thinker and guide of popes and of the Medici
of the Renaissance, transformed human dignity based upon the hope
of overcoming falleness into something quite different. "The fathers
of the Church had placed man in a dignified position," Yates writes,
"as the highest of terrestrial beings, as spectator of the universe, as
the microcosm containing within himself the reflection of the mac-
rocosm." But Pico's oration goes a step further. "All these orthodox
notions are in the oration on the Dignity of Man," but these ideas are
used to support the notion of the human being as "Magus, as operator,
having within him the divine creative power, and the magical power
of marrying heaven and earth" with the anticipation that since once
human beings held such powers, they could once again become the
masters of nature through the intellect, and this new Man could come
into his proper role as "a divine being."[4]

"Science as a Vocation"

That such speculation about the nature of humanity was given to
many subtle, and not so subtle, variations is to be expected. Yet it is
only by virtue of its long usage in modern times that we fail to recognize that the rhetoric of the Renaissance, carried to even greater
extremes in the Enlightenment, has exaggerated beyond measure the
orthodox Christian view that, while the human beings are preeminent
in nature, they nevertheless participate in nature as fellow creatures in
a created order. The strong Christian sentiment of the human being's
endowed preeminence in nature is now parleyed into a rightful claim
to power *over* nature. Baconian themes of the reordering of existence
are mirrored in the system building of Descartes, which promised a

science to bring mankind into their proper role as "the masters and possessors of nature."

These notions were hardly isolated and transient expressions of enthusiasm in an adolescent Europe. Three centuries later we find them expressed with undiminished force, even if each generation hears them as something absolutely new. A powerful example is the impact of a certain early twentieth century address by Max Weber. This address, as a matter of fact, could be seen as a contemporary updating and re-framing of Pico della Mirandella's oration. Like its Renaissance prototype, Weber's address is a peculiar blend of science and theology.

In 1919, Weber was invited to give an address to students on "Science as a Vocation." This address comes down to us as both a very strange essay and an extraordinarily influential one. The influence of the piece speaks for itself. It has fostered a way of thinking about our world and the place of formal studies in that world that remains a strong prejudice in contemporary thinking. And I mean by "prejudice" not blind bigotry as it has come to be used, but a settled conviction that, as Edmund Burke said, is necessary to conversations of a very high order. And when I say that it is "strange," I am not suggesting that it is merely eccentric and for that reason easily dismissed. I happen hold to the rather conventional view that Max Weber is one of the most formidable intellectuals of the past century. As Leo Strauss said, "Whatever may have been his errors, he is the greatest social scientist of our century." What I mean by strange is that it is profoundly ironic. It seems to advance the cause of modern science only by resurrecting the theology of polytheism. He properly sees that the questions of "meaning" raised by modern science are necessarily theological questions. But rather than attempt to answer those questions—which he admits science is incapable of doing—he said that "the different value systems of the world stand in conflict with one another."[5] The religious journey of the world that has led to monotheism, as well as mono-ethics, and which "dethroned this polytheism in favor of 'the One that is necessary'" has been faced with new contingencies in a modern world. He could as easily have said that the rationalizing and disenchantment of the world that are by-products of monotheism have now become superannuated; but because of an extraordinary reversal of world views, we must abandon monotheism and along with it, mono-ethics. What he did say was that "just as Hellenic man sacrificed on this occasion to Aphrodite and on another to Apollo, and above all as everybody sacrificed to the gods of his city—things are still the same today, but disenchanted and divested of the mythical but inwardly genuine flexibility of those customs." For instance, he argues,

> What man would presume to "refuse scientifically" the morality of the Sermon on the Mount, for example the sentence "resist no evil" or the image of turning the other cheek? And yet it is clear from the perspective of this world that here an undignified morality is being preached. The choice is between the religious dignity which this morality confers and the dignity of man, which preaches something quite different; "Resist evil, for otherwise you will share the responsibility for its supremacy." For each individual, according to his ultimate standpoint, one is the devil and the other God, and the individual must decide which *for him* is God and which the devil. And so it is in all aspects of life.[6]

It is no wonder, then, that he quotes John Stuart Mill favorably to the effect that "if one proceeds from pure experience, one arrives at polytheism."[7] It is also important to see that the idea of vocation tends toward monotheism, as does the idea of liberal arts which always refers back to first principles and to higher unifying ideals. What is described here is the abstract design of a multicultural world view, where "different value systems of the world stand in conflict with one another."[8]

It is serendipitous, from the standpoint of a researcher into culture and the sources of community, that in this essay a major shaper of modern thought brings together the issues of higher education, the vocation of human beings as "knowers" (scientists), and the meaning of the human community.[9] It is remarkable, further, that we have at hand an oration (that of Pico della Mirandella) appearing at the dawn, rather than at the decadent end, of modernity that reflects upon these same issues in rather comparable ways. In between, we have an abundance of evidence that the rhetoric of the divine powers and privileges of the human being works no matter how preposterous the form in which it comes to us. And preposterous is not too strong a term to describe Emerson's *Nature* or Kant's invitation for every man to think for himself, or Locke's presumption in making a *tabula rasa* (as Eric Voegelin put it) of two thousand years of Christian intellectual history, replacing it with "an analysis of the New Testament as if it were a book that had been published yesterday."[10]

"Vocation" at the heart of community

What is missing is not the simple idea of community, about which postmodernists never tire of speaking. Rather, the distinction that needs to come to light more clearly is the nature of that body, whether it is based on "love," and the longing for a higher unity—a basis for communing—or whether it is based on "equality" expressed as rights, which is a kind of calculation. In one, the person is indispensable. In the other the individual is interchangeable, for if all are equal in every way, one will do as well as the other. But if we belong in different ways and for different purposes to the same body, then our gifts are needed and our lives are valued precisely because we are different.

The distinction here is highlighted once again when we detect the theological idea of *vocatio* in the aesthetic experience, in the experience of beauty. One who experiences beauty, as Josef Pieper and Franz

Rosenzweig explain, does not experience perfection but the provoking of a suffering for what is perfect. That is why the encounter with that which is perceived by us as beautiful is accompanied by a measure of "suffering" or "pain" which we might express as longing, even if it is accompanied by what we would call "joy." Just so, the one who is "called" and experiences life as a "call" can be said to suffer for that which is higher, nobler, better. It is the experience of love, hope, faith, the theological virtues: each of which expresses a certain "longing for" and a certain "suffering for" that which is unknown in the sense of having "mastered" it, but known in the sense that it has laid hold of our affections and our intellectual anticipation. It is unknown as a possession, but in an ineffable way it has taken possession of the one who has perceived beauty. It is known not as something subject to one's power, but as the object of one's longing and suffering love.

Beauty can thus be experienced in a way very much like vocation. The antagonism between beauty as that which beckons us further and whets our appetite for more and beauty as mere taste and personal preference mirrors the tension between two competing visions of community life, and two contrary ideas of what forms community. These rivals have not emerged in modern times; it is only that their rivalry has been clarified as never before. The options between them have always been present, and as a prudential matter, they will be present until the final judgment. It is the rivalry between power in the sense of force as the means of social organization, and affection as the tie that binds people together, that binds them to their proper tasks, that binds them in creative and loving ways to their places and their things. The important thing to see is that both of these principles have their place, practically speaking, in the world as we know it. Power as coercion has its place because the world is fallen. The power of affection or love has its place because the world longs for redemption. Yet they are competing options, and each appeals to us with ecumenical designs; both are ambitious in an empire-building way, seeking to complete itself with world domination.

The Christian hope is that love will win out, binding everything together in a web of divine *vocatio*—all things called to their proper place in a celebration where it is possible to

> Let the sea roar, and all that fills it;
> The world and those who live in it.
> Let the floods clap their hands;
> Let the hills sing together for joy . . . .[11]

And because this *vocatio*, this call, has affected the world so strongly, it has often played into the hands of the rival, for force offers immediacy, it short-circuits those features of vocation which are characterized by a suffering-longing, a resistance to distraction, and a quest that leads into an eternal mystery. Power is the siren call that offers relief from the suffering of love. But power as force also proves the truth of Kafka's fifty-word story entitled *The Sirens*: "These are the seductive voices of the night; the Sirens, too, sang that way. It would be doing them an injustice to think that they wanted to seduce; they knew they had claws and sterile wombs, and they lamented this aloud. They could not help it if their laments sounded so beautiful."[12]

In a fallen world, power as force or coercion is needed as a prophylactic against violence. And though it is always sterile and unproductive of those virtues most needed in the social life, it tempts us to believe that it can accomplish quickly what love does only through patience and only fully accomplishes at the End of All Things. The generating influence of this sentiment that lies so deeply within us, and which we call "vocation" out of a certain loss for knowing quite what to call it, is a constant reminder that something besides human choice defines the true nature of those ties that bind a people together and to their world.

4

The Decline of Vocation

I F THE MODERN WORLD is strongly marked by its love of power—that is, its love of the kind of power that controls through science, technology, organization and so on—then the decline of the sentiment of vocation can be traced with a fair degree of certainty. The stages of this recession are not surprising, though the extremity in which it has manifested itself (and the real name of that extremity) is something modern people would generally reject, although they, more than any other peoples of any other age are most acquainted with it. I will begin with the historical and cultural background; and then (since to do so immediately might prove more shocking than edifying) I will attempt to call things by their proper names.

The sixteenth and seventeenth centuries brought impressive advances in technology, or—to use plainer language—in the use of implements or tools to accomplish practical tasks. This advance was so impressive and made such a remarkable impact upon society that a number of direct or indirect consequences made themselves felt.

First, progress in technology suggested that progress was a general rule in human experience and that it was a force that operated throughout social, moral, and artistic life; that what was the rule for technology was also the rule for civilization and culture, bringing all things under the power of an unseen evolutionary hand. What was evidently true in the limited field of technology, and what had been the eschatological focus of the Church's teachings—teachings in the final triumph of a divine order—joined in the Western mind to create the first secular myth of automatic and inexorable progress.

Second, the increased use of technology drew larger numbers of people to centers of production and commerce, giving rise to the phenomenal growth of urban living and the ready availability of manpower for industry and army, for production and conquest.

Third, the labor force, the government, and the army developed along lines analogous to the machine, rather than the organic vision of agrarian society. In the latter, the persons of a community were indispensable, or nearly so, members of a body in which they played their role by virtue of gifs peculiar to each—one a farmer, another a blacksmith, another a warrior, yet another responsible for nurturing the young. In the former, it became best to view so-called individuals as "equals." Thus, like parts of a machine they were also interchangeable and answerable not so much to the peculiarity of their gifts and their contribution to society at large, but answerable to an increasingly centralized and efficient organization of mankind dedicated to the twin sources of the phenomenal wealth now attending the urban growth: production and conquest.

Fourth, similarly, governments were organized for the efficient administration of large territories and the gradual yet effective opposition to barriers (including and sometimes especially the moral and religious ones) that hampered profitable enterprises. One can see this especially in the effort (beginning with Locke) to distinguish between a public and private realm, in which matters of moral and religious concern were relegated to the private, where the influence of church and family could not discourage free rein in the public realm of commercial enterprise. By such logic, the slave trade was newly and vigorously introduced into Western commerce and the former depredations of the church were blunted, as we shall see.

Fifth, social organization increasingly imitated the rational use of implements—of machines.

Sixth, consequently, the social consciousness of large territories began to be formed less around communities that depended directly upon the land and were place-oriented, and that had supported the same families and monasteries for generations. Now that consciousness shifted ever so slightly and gradually (though exponentially through the twentieth century) toward those urban centers of manufacture, trade, and government (growth industries all!) where the power of technology and bureaucratic organization could be felt in its full force.

Along with these changes—and a number of others including the all-important rise of banks, currency, and joint-stock ownership of commercial enterprises (beginning with the English East India Company in 1600)—came a number of reflexive changes, changes in the way men, women, and children saw themselves. First, and of radical importance, was the inevitable sense that something more or less permanent no longer undergirded, nourished, and protected them: the land to which they belonged, and that was the common environment of all—rich and poor, old and young, from birth to death—was in smaller and smaller measure the environment that determined the shape of their lives. In its place was the city, organized and functioning as a market and a center of power.

Formerly one could say that men thought of themselves as "belonging" to the land, which exercised a benevolent and relatively predictable influence over their lives. Later thy would belong to a company, or to a standing army, or to the state—each jealously guarding its prerogatives against human associations such as the family, the church, the region, the tribe or clan, and the guild—gradually reaching an apogee in the twentieth century, when it was possible to view the individual as belonging wholly to a totalitarian state. A totalitarian state is nothing other than a state that has absorbed all other civilizing and human loyalties so that the individual belongs exclusively to the state.

Unlike the land, the state and commercial enterprises, along with the large armed and disciplined military that protected their ambitions over rival cities and territories, were not relatively predictable in their influence, as was the land, but high unpredictable. The efforts to rein in these arbitrary powers is the story of the modern growth of liberty, but it is also the story of the modern loss of independence for individuals who were once sheltered by their social institutions that were ancient and venerable—such as the family and church—but existed for purposes that far transcended commerce and power.

Part of this story is the story of liberty and points to an important—perhaps the most important—achievement of modern times. That is, modernity has seen the culmination of millennia of development in recognition of the dignity of the individual. Where such a development was balanced, it recognized that without the value of the person there is no real possibility of community. But where the emphasis on the individual was unbalanced by the fanciful dreams of Renaissance and Enlightenment thinkers and social movements, it became a detriment to community. That, unfortunately, is where we find ourselves at the moment. When liberty becomes an abstract cause, broken off from the holistic meaning of the person living with others, it becomes as narrow as the cause it represents—whether that cause be labor, filial rights, women's liberation, animal rights, or any one of the many causes which now occupy the contemporary mind. This, we ought to note, is an abstraction that represents a considerable decline from the earlier calling together of community in the Christian experience of people living a life of mutual service and love. In this earlier experience, all of the person's life is called upon in community with others. In the modern movements, celebrated and animated as causes, the character and the talents of the person is eclipsed by the requirements of the cause itself, calling instead upon the person in the narrowest and most abstract sense.[1] The community drawn together, made up of whole persons, in particular circumstances, by the charismatic power of the Spirit, is always concrete and historical. Those called together in the modern age, on the basis of "cause" are inevitably abstract and only historical perhaps in the sense of the ideology of 'historical forces' of which the Marxists and fascists were so fond of speaking, while they were dividing Europe (as Bernard-Henri Levy said) like "two great black birds" that plagued the middle of the last century.

In that it was indeed and authentically the story of liberty—from the Magna Carta to the Declaration of Independence—it betrays a certain resistance to the growing stream of history propelled by new possibilities for power and material ambition, a possibility emerging chiefly from technology: the enhancement and extension of the human will. That is, authentic calls for liberty will always recognize the importance of natural communities—not bureaucracies, states, armies, and corporations, but families, cities, friendships, collegial associations—as the mainstay of the private person's liberty from unwanted intrusions upon the very things that give life its meaning in community.

Second, the human being who saw himself, over time, and more so in some locations than others, as "belonging" to the "state" or to the "company" found it impossible to recover the secure sense of belonging to the land. "Belong" in these two distinct contexts implies entirely different things about the nature and the moral relationships of people in community. To belong to the land means that in many important ways one participates in a creation that includes, influences, sustains, nurtures, and embraces in a thousand different ways all men equally, regardless of rank or station, regardless of sex or age. But to belong to a "company," let us say, means that one is subject to the will of another and in some ways is sustained only by the arbitrary good will of others. It implies that one belongs in a way that is not true of a family or a church, for this "belonging" is made possible by the activity and initiative of those who are in positions of power.

Medieval kings depended upon the land as much as anyone else and thus belonged to the land no less and no more than yeomen who worked the land. Yet, for all of the modern emphasis on equality, nothing undermined the sentiment of equality more than the bureaucratic state, the army it maintained, organized by ranks for efficient control in battle, and the company organized for the practical tasks of commercial conquests.

I must pause at this point to reassure the reader that I am not envisioning—or suggesting in any way—some sort of return to a time innocent of technological sophistication, or an Amish-like resistance to technology. I mean only to convey the reality that these rich blessings of modern technology inevitably brought with them a new sentiment, new way in which the increasingly urbanized man could begin to think about himself. In early modernity, it begins to appear in forms that were starkly out of harmony with the moral sentiment that was introduced along with Christianity. In later years the same forms were not so much eradicated as disguised or submerged in a culture that—at least at the rhetorical level—valued liberty. Yet modernity itself is hardly conceivable without these new forms of human relations. For man had become increasingly an instrument for production, profit, and warfare. Rather than a participant in a creation that embraced all men equally, and that required a common seeking after the good of a community, this new relationship implied something else. It implied that the naked purpose of existence was production, conquest, and material acquisition—a purpose that indeed sanctified power and possession, rooted somehow in the mystery of pleasure—but a purpose expressive of the human will and its capacity for acquisition and domination.

Thus human relationships in modern times were over time transformed from that of a "community" in which men troubled themselves with the common good, to a community in name only: a consensus of individuals under obligation to an organized, rather than an organic, society. There was no longer any moral object or aesthetic judgment or divine creator that was the subject of their "communing." Instead the task that lay before them was self-evident: production and conquest. Albert Camus powerfully proved, in his essay on the sources of human violence and enslavement, that "the myth of unlimited production" to which we are drawn by the spectacular (though still limited) success of modern techno-science "brings war in its train as inevitably as clouds announce a storm."[2]

Slavery: the eldest child of modernity

We have already seen how the modern, increasingly urbanized, technologically sophisticated, society had become organized in a way congenial to the uses of power and material acquisitiveness. The usefulness of human beings in this relationship was made more feasible when they were understood as equals in the modern sense—that is, as interchangeable units in a machine—and fundamentally alienated from natural associations, "belonging" only in the new, modern sense.

This new relationship is only adequately articulated, as we shall see, by the master-slave language, though this language—thanks to the pre-modern influence of Christianity—is highly offensive, causing modern people to reject the system of slavery when it is visibly evident (as in the plantation systems of the early U.S.) and to submerge it in forms that are less visible (such as in trade arrangements with China where slave labor is employed, or in the public worship of the rich, and the famous, and the powerful).

It is often thought that the modern rejection of slavery was part and parcel of the new enlightenment of man as he emerged from the "darkness" of earlier times. Yet a closer look at the institution can show why and how slavery was more the child of modernity than it was ever the product of ancient and medieval Christendom.

Two features of slavery—its transforming of a human being into an instrument for use, a resource for the masters of the larger society, and its destruction or at least neglect of natural relations within natural groups such as the family and clan and leaving in its place the alienated individual—are also features of modernity. Within the history of slavery we shall always find these two features prominent; it is no wonder that early modern leaders of the Enlightenment nearly always defended and promoted slavery. They were above all promoting the instrumentalizing of the individual and the individualizing (that is, the alienating from natural relations) of the *human* instruments of labor.

The first feature—the human as instrument—requires little of our attention. It is a classical Aristotelian definition of the slave, that he is "part of the master, a living but separated part of his bodily frame." He is thus an extension, like any other tool or instrument, only he is a living instrument.[3] The degree to which human beings are turned conceptually into utilitarian objects has possibly never reached such clear expression until the twentieth century, when government and corporation bureaus began to be named "Office of Human Resources." Yet slavery was, and is, in effect reducing the human to the status of a living tool—one who serves purposes for others, and who does not find value in himself as a worthy object of love and dignity.

Helmut Thielicke, the great German pastor and theologian, saw this conceptual reduction having dire effects upon the German mind in the early part of the twentieth century. "How did the Holocaust occur?" he was asked. There were many reasons—some economic and political. But at base, the people had forgotten a fundamental teaching of the Christian idea of man, one that Martin Luther had called his alien dignity. That is, the human being found his value not in some intrinsic "beauty," or "usefulness" to society, but in the fact that he is created by God, the object of God's redemptive work, and is loved by God. Thus even those who are very young, very old, very sick, perhaps invalid or mentally defective, still retain the dignity that comes from God's own disposition toward them. It was when the popular mind was infected with the notion that one's value came from one's usefulness to the greater society that the inhuman philosophies could take root: those that rid society first of the old and defective, then of the unborn, and finally of the Jews and other scapegoats of the Nazi regime.

With the second feature—the individualizing (alienation) of human existence—we have made the full descent. It has been a descent from an idea of vocation that evokes the human person in his full connectedness, as a social being with responsibilities, loves, and a fully social understanding of himself: not as mere free agent with an isolated and unhindered will, but as father, mother, brother, daughter, colleague, neighbor, and friend, each with its peculiar role, obligations, and sentiments.

The Enlightenment and post-enlightenment ideas of emancipation play a role. For as long as the free man is defined as one who pursues his own will, the man with social obligations to family, church, tribe, region, and tradition, might be made to feel a certain resentment. And the more he is free of these "petty obligations" the more he might be *useful* to the larger interests of nation-states and international corporations. He becomes an instrument; but more deeply important is that he is freed from what Tennessee Williams called those "tender bonds" that tie us to a less regimented and organized social group that can only hamper the work of a society based on production and conquest.

To understand why slavery was at first—and remains in a hidden way—so appealing to the modern mind, we have to understand that at the heart of it is the recasting of the human image in ways that are useful because they are alienated from what might, at earlier times, be taken for the benefits of tender bonds. Sociologists sometimes refer to these as "mediating institutions," a term that seems to imply the secondary role of church and family, for instance, in the life of the individual and the state.

It is difficult to describe the modern emergence of slavery without first correcting the popular notion that slavery was gradually overcome by the forces of Enlightenment, having survived antiquity and the Middle Ages due to the ignorance in whch the world was held bondage. The true picture is much more complicated than can be presented here, but fundamentally the Christian lands first yielded to the pressure of the Church in its prohibition of slavery. Slave trade and slave holding went into eclipse for more than half of a millennium. The invective of the Church against slavery was severe. Early adherents of Christianity (a "slave religion," as it was called by the Romans) convincingly preached that Christian anthropology did not permit slavery or any such traffic in human flesh. Gregory of Nyssa serves as an example of the strength of Christian opposition to slavery.

Commenting on Ecclesiastes 2:7, to the effect that "I acquired slaves and slave girls, and slaves were born in my house," he makes his case against the holding of slaves:

> Does any of the things listed here, a sumptuous house, vineyards galore, beautiful gardens, a system of pools supplying orchards with water, suggest as much arrogance as the man's idea that he as a man can be master over his fellows? "For I acquired," he says, "slaves and slave girls, and slaves were born in my house." Do you see the vast extent of his boastfulness? Such a voice as his is raised in open defiance against God. . . .
>
> "I have acquired slaves and slave girls." What is that you say? You condemn a person to slavery whose nature is free and independent, and in doing so you lay down a law in opposition to God, overturning the natural law established by him. For you subject to the yoke of slavery one who was created precisely to

be a master of the earth, and who was ordained to rule by the creator, as if you were deliberately attacking and fighting against the divine command. . . .

"I acquired slaves and slave girls." Tell me, what price did you pay for them? What did you find among your possessions that you could trade for human beings? What price did you put on reason? How many obols did you pay as a fair price for the image of God? For how many staters have you sold the nature specially formed by God? "God said, 'Let us make man in our image and likeness.'" Tell me this: who can buy a man, who can sell him, when he is made in the likeness of God, when he is ruler over the whole earth, when he has been given as his inheritance by God authority over all that is on the earth? Such power belongs to God alone, or rather it does not even belong to God himself. For, as Scripture says, "the gifts of God are irrevocable." Of his own free will God called us into freedom when we were slaves to sin. In that case he would hardly reduce human beings to slavery. But if God does not enslave what is free, who dares put his own authority higher than God's? . . . .

When a man is put up for sale, nothing less than the lord of the earth is led onto the auction block. . . .[4]

Such strong sentiments could only be overcome by madness. And madness was plentifully supplied in an age, corresponding to the Enlightenment, in which the new Western lands were being discovered and the vision of immense wealth and power coaxed Europe from its historic faith, in an age of vast trade, powerful armies, new sciences, and heady secular possibilities.

It is necessary to see that slavery was not extinguished with the so-called Enlightenment, but in fact just the opposite. Along with the rise of urban centers and the development of nation-states, and along with new opportunities in transatlantic lands, the slave trade took on new life. First Portugal, then England, New England, and Holland became wealthy by it. Pope Leo x (1513-22) had declared in a bull that "not only the Chrsitian religion, but nature herself, cried out against the system of slavery."[5] Nevertheless, the slave trade increased each decade through most of the sixteenth and seventeenth centuries. By early in the eighteenth century, the English slave-merchants alone were transporting fifteen thousand persons per year out of Africa, and by 1733, the figure had increased to twenty thousand. In *Fruits of Merchant Capital,* Elizabeth Fox-Genovese and Eugene Genovese reveal the anomaly of modern capitalism which "rested on free labor and had no meaning apart from it," while at the same time it created new "servile systems" wherever it arose "including systems of chattel slavery, on an unprecedented social scale and at an unprecedented level of violence."[6]

David Brion Davis demonstrates that the earliest modern attitude toward slavery was that it was a feature of the general "progressive" nature of things. It was seen as part and parcel of the modern age. Like many other advances in science, politics, and trade, it promised great wealth in the new age a-dawning. In the New World, Davis shows, "it is clear that black slavery was indispensable not only for regions capable of producing agricultural staples but also for the port cities and neighboring commercial farms and livestock-raising centers from Newport to Buenos Aires."[7] There was, during the first two hundred years of the modern period, no division into "free industrial and plantation mentality" of the Americas. The slave population of New England, the middle colonies, and the southern colonies all grew apace. At times, in North America, the colonies of the North outgrew those of the South in terms of slave holding: "In 1690, the proportion of slaves in the northern port towns still approximated that in tobacco-growing Virginia and Maryland, and greatly exceeded that in North Carolina."[8] While there was a level of resistance to the idea of slavery throughout the Americas, the economic advantage of slavery began to increase in the Southern colonies and in the Caribbean, and to decline elsewhere.

Only gradually did this "modern" obsession change with regard to slavery. The horrors that took place in the Caribbean did their part in awakening the consciences of Christians everywhere. There were anti-slave movements throughout the Western hemisphere. St. George Tucker, a Virginian, one of the most highly respected jurists in America, was outspoken in this regard. David Brion Davis wrote that "until the 1760s, roughly speaking, black slavery was generally assumed to be a necessary and 'progressive' institution, accepted or tolerated in cities like Boston, New York, and London, which were far removed from the booming peripheral zones of plantation agriculture."[9]

The trade in human flesh, even before this time, did not go unchallenged. Often, on the local level, it was resisted, but continued to be supported by the sovereigns of the new nation-states, whose interests were more attuned to the rising commercial class. In 1760, for instance, South Carolina attempted to prohibit the further importation of slaves, but the act was vetoed by the Crown. Virginia petitioned the Crown on four occasions to stop the slave trade on the Virginia shores, but was repeatedly turned down by a government under much pressure from business interests at home. Thomas Jefferson originally intended to list this action in the *Declaration of Independence* along with the other offenses against the colonies, but withdrew it when it became apparent that doing so would prove offensive to Massachusetts and South Carolina. The original intention of the framers of the American Constitution was to end slave trade by 1800, but the measure was put off until 1808 by a motion put forward by South Carolina and seconded by Massachusetts.

In England, finally it was a largely religious movement led by notable Christians—especially William Wilberforce and John Wesley—that brought both slave-trading and slave-holding to an end in the British empire. In 1834, at the stroke of a pen, three-quarters of a million slaves were set free, and the owners were compensated with 20 million sterling. And, of course, the issue was settled in a rather more costly fashion in the United States and in a way that affirmed, rather than denied, the commercial interests of the dominant party.

It is common to think of the "slave" as the counterpart of the autonomous person, the free worker in the industrial and commercial market. Actually, for most of history, and among most peoples in history, the slave is one who specifically did no longer belong to the family, or to his own people, but belonged to a stranger. It might be said without exaggeration that everyone was thought to "belong" to someone, or to some family or group. But when one belongs to strangers, the misfortune is described by the status of "slave." Early Hebrews were restricted from making slaves of their own people; and if one of them had become so indebted that they sold themselves into slavery to foreigners, their next of kin was obliged to buy them back, to "redeem" them.[10] This meant, of course, they were restored to their "proper" belonging, not restored to autonomous self-ownership. In fact, there was no such thing.

David Brion Davis, points out that in early Saxon law "the 'autonomous' stranger who had no family or clan to protect him was automatically regarded as a slave." The same sort of concept operated in most African nations, where the opposite of slavery is not "'freedom' qua autonomy but rather 'belonging.'" Davis gives the example of the terms used by Giriama, one of the Kenyan peoples. There the term for slave is *mtumwa*. When asked for a contrary term, the native person would reply that a non-slave is simply one of the Giriama people. Thus, Davis says, in premodern societies "the salient characteristic of slavery was its antithetical relation to the normal network of kinship ties of dependency, protection, obligation, and privilege, ties that easily served as a model of nonkinship forms of patronage, clientage, and voluntary servitude."[11] "In a sense," Davis maintains, "slaves were the first 'modern' people."[12]

Orlando Patterson defined slavery this way: "The essence of slavery is that the slave, in his social death, lives on the margin between community and chaos, life and death, the sacred and the secular."[13] It is not "working for the benefit of another" that makes a person a slave; that much we might all wish to do. But it is having *no real community* for which to work: to be alienated, living as an alien, engaged not as a human but, in Aristotle's language, as a "tool" of others. There is a sense in which the "machinery of production" or the bureaucracy—that artifice of human beings organized for efficient production—is best served, as Patterson remarks, by "natally alienated persons who could most readily be employed in this way: ever ready to move physically, and occupationally, not only upward but laterally, downward, and out; ever ready to retrain for entirely new positions and to accept, without complaint, whatever was offered in remuneration."[14] It is not as if their conditions are equivalent, of course, but in terms of these "useful" considerations, this might just as well describe the modern middle class worker and bureaucrat as it does the nineteenth century agrarian slave.

Davis also indicates the place at which slavery and modern bureaucracy are joined: the "'modernity' of the slave lay in his continuing marginality and vulnerability, in his incomplete and ambiguous bonding to a social group." Thus, "as a replaceable and interchangeable outsider faced with the unpredictable need of adjusting to wholly alien cultures, he was the prototype for the migratory labor and confused identity that have accompanied every phrase of human progress."[15] This is why I introduced "slavery" as a sort of marker of the growth of the modern sentiment. While explicit forms of slavery *never* found a comfortable home in the West once Christianity had taken root, it was reintroduced and then took on more and more subtle forms until today one is hardly aware of how strongly society is organized to benefit the few at the expense of the many who are routinely uprooted and who remain "alien residents" in a society organized for the masters of commerce and government—what, in its more explicit form, is called slavery.

There is much discussion about whether the American Civil War was indeed over the issue of slavery, or over other issues for which slavery became a convenient excuse, in Lincoln's government, to take the moral high ground, thus discouraging England and France from siding with the Confederacy. It could more accurately be said that the real struggle was over replacing the feudal form of slavery in the South with the more modern form of slavery represented by the mercantilism and imperial ambitions of the North. Once the United States was consolidated into a unitary governmental system ("One nation, indivisible") as in Western Europe, it was not long before the campaign to subjugate the aboriginal population was in full heat, with some who helped free the slaves declaring, as did General Sherman, that "the only good Indians I ever saw were dead."[16] And it was not forty years before the United States was at war with Spain, asserting its hegemony over the Philippines at the cost of 250,000 Filipino lives.

Most, therefore, think of slavery as a thing of the past, and the attempt to tie the institution to the recent past—say the past century or so—meets with steely resistance. We tend not to listen. Such notions we have learned to associate with strident ideologies: two generations of Marxist rhetoric have made us skeptical. Yet there are those we should heed. It is true that we no longer have the visible institution of domestic slavery such as existed in the nineteenth century, especially but not exclusively in the American South. But when some populations are living sumptuously at the expense of others who are barely able to feed their young, is that not also slavery, one might ask? Or when large populations live as "alien residents"—which was a biblical term practically equivalent to "slaves"—then are there not some remaining signs of the institution? When so many people are heavily in debt, and some third world nations as well, can they truly be said to work for their own living? Or do they, just as in any ancient slave system, work for the primary benefit of others—even for others they do not know? This latter-day slave system has the convenience of remaining out of sight, and thus unoffensive to a sensitive bourgeois population.

Jürgen Moltmann sees a close tie between the earlier "visible" slavery and the later and more enduring form of slavery. Modernity, he says, spawned *submodernity*: "History's fine messianic top coat has its ugly apocalyptic underside." This is the meaning of what we call the "Third World" whose sufferings in part reflect the spectacular gains of the "First World." It was "only the modern mass enslavement of Africans and the exploitation of America's mineral resources which provided the labour and capital for the development and advancement of the West." Well into the nineteenth century, Europe's wealth was built up on the basis of a great transcontinental, triangular commerce: slaves from Africa to America; gold and silver from America to Europe, followed by sugar, cotton, coffee, tobacco and rubber; then industrial commodities and weapons to Africa; and so on. Thus was produced the wealth, the industrial capital, and the enormous trading advantages of Western Europe. "Through slave trade it destroyed the cultures and kingdoms of West Africa, and through monocultures it wrecked the native subsistence economies of Central and South America, making whole peoples the victims of European development."[17]

Beginning with the early modern slave trade and moving forward in time, Moltmann would not argue that the situation improved, but in fact got worse. "The exploited Third World is being turned into a superfluous backwoods, and its population into 'surplus people'. We see the first sign of this road to exterminism in 'the coming anarchy' in Africa, the forgotten continent . . . . West African states are disintegrating and becoming ungovernable. Power is no longer a monopoly of the state. The ecological destruction of the countryside is driving people into the slums of the big cities. Malaria and AIDS are turning more and more people into lepers. The plagues are coming back."[18]

When much of the Third World was under colonial rule from European nations, they were subjected to an alien regime, and thus unable to sustain their own native culture—including agriculture—in the way handed down over time and refined by community habits. The whole fabric of culture was cut to fit the new regime and no longer worked in the same way as before. Then when colonial rule was lifted, the multifaceted nature of colonial rule was withdrawn, but the narrow economic interests remained, so that the form of dependence became more, rather than less, impersonal. It became an abstract rather than a concrete and holistic regime. The indebtedness of the former colonial peoples meant that the burden of working for others (theoretically until the debt was paid) was no less; but the absence of the kinds of institutions earlier provided along with colonial rule, meant that the kinds of supports that came with the economic interests as well as the rule of a foreign people were no longer there. Now they were making bricks without straw—only in the form of having to meet economic demands without cultural support. It might have been better to have had their own native cultural institutions than to be subject to alien forms; but it was better to have the foreign institutions than to have none at all that could match the level of economic demands being made upon them. Beside this, the earlier domestic slavery in America might even have been more benign.

5

Distraction

MY WIFE'S FAMILY IS FROM APPALACHIA, that part of it at the western-most end of North Carolina known as the Smoky Mountains. Her father, both before retirement from public work and after, was a skilled cabinet maker. His customers often came from considerable distances and went to some amount of trouble in order to employ him for making a table, a kitchen cabinet, a chest-of-drawers, a gun cabinet, and so on.

Once he took me out to his workshop to show me one of his latest projects. It was a rather heavy, ornate, desk—the kind with a roll-top enclosure that pulls over a bank of pigeon holes at the back and a smooth writing surface at the forward half, all of which can be closed and locked when the roll-top is pulled into place. The desk was still unstained. It was made of a light-colored oak, almost white, and had drawers on either side as well as one in the front center.

"Let me show you something," he said. Placing one finger under the pull of a side drawer, he drew the heavy piece out effortlessly. Then he removed the drawer to show me that there were no steel tracks or ball bearings. All of the drawers performed the same: no gimmicks, they fit perfectly in place. "I didn't have to go to that much trouble," he said, "but then Alec (his customer on this occasion) wouldn't ask me to do anything else for him."

This last remark came along with a certain twinkle in the eye that let me know he had in mind more than simple "customer satisfaction." The severest critic stood there at my elbow—the proud craftsman, not the relatively indifferent buyer.

Such a feat in the artistry of cabinet making, however subtle and hidden, required attitudes and disciplines that are not distinguishing marks of modernity. In fact, they help us to mark off the line of habits and thought that do seem to distinguish our age and its culture. Patience and a willingness to use time in order to improve a piece of work is what might immediately come to mind. This kind of investment, furthermore, takes into account the features of the particular material with which the skilled craftsman is working—the hardness or softness of the wood, the capacity of the wood for expansion, plus any peculiar flaws in the wood. The worker also considers his own skills, pushing them to the limit, but also subtly working around whatever might be lacking in skill or in the availability of tools. The craftsman is intensely interested in the peculiarities of *this* material, *this* design, and the circumstances of this attempt at fashioning something both useful and beautiful.

Modern life, in contrast to these preoccupations, is absorbed with the task of making more with less. Markets, in the early modern period—no earlier than the fourteenth century, nor later that the sixteenth—expanded dramatically. They increased due to more reliable long-distance travel, the exploration of new regions, the growth of European population, and the domination by central governments of ever larger regions—the so-called emergence of the nation-states. This latter development had a homogenizing effect. Rather than Picts and Scots, Angles and Saxons, Normans and Welsh, they all were governed by the British Crown. The same sort of thing was taking place in France and Spain, and would later take place in Italy and Germany.

It was a tendency that by now has spanned the globe: mass governments and mass markets—for very good reason—grew up together.
Ethnic distinctions were counterproductive in mass markets: the less
important the distinctions, the more products moved easily to a consequently larger population.

Therefore attention moved by degrees from that of perfecting a
single piece of work to that of reproducing that work with less cost.
Reproduction called for understanding things abstractly more than
concretely. It is not the nature of this piece of wood that is needed
so much as the nature of this *kind* of wood—not the nature of this
craftsman, but the nature of the *average* worker—not the circumstances of producing *this* one piece, but the conditions by which a
continual flow of production can take place. A hundred and some
odd miles to the east of this simple mountain workshop the furniture
mills of central Carolina steadily produce well-designed furniture,
but operating on a very different principle and from fundamentally
different motives. They are in fact modern motives. They are modern
in that they are more abstract: the successful business is known by its
"bottom line"—in other words, by an abstractly articulated monetary
value, a value that is tenuously related to the value of the product as
furniture or as art. For the modern world, a thing becomes of value
in a way that is rationally divorced from the thing itself, while in the
traditional society the value is worked *into* the object and becomes
identified with the object itself. Similarly, the beauty of a product is
(for the modern) in the design rather than in the thing itself.

The end toward which the modern craftsman works, therefore,
is removed from the thing itself. He makes furniture, but *for the sake
of* making money. The means by which one works becomes more
important than the end product, whether the intention is to produce
a piece of furniture, or an automobile, or to cure a patient, or to
render justice in the courts. The design, an abstraction of the thing
itself, is the object of attention. Thus we attend to the abstraction of

money, or design, of means, of power—of all manner of things that bear some relationship to what is the apparent object of our work, but not the object itself.

We are distracted. To be modern is to exist increasingly in a state of distraction. Our attention is drawn away from those things that have been placed in our care, away from the center of our apparent concern to something abstractly related to that concern, and thus away from God himself who is the center of all things. To be modern is not only to find ourselves thus distracted, but to justify that life of distraction. In this sense, the problem of modernity is not so much an intellectual problem, and not basically an intellectual problem: it is rather a moral problem and a problem of the affections. We have failed to love properly what we ought to love and we fall away from that love which draws us toward God. Instead we fasten upon that which draws us away from God.

The Marks of Modernity

When we test this idea of "distraction" against the typical way of explaining the Enlightenment and its character, I think we shall see that the two are not that far apart. Let me take as an example an excellent essay by Theodore M. Greene that serves as an introduction to a standard contemporary edition of Kant's *Religion Within the Limits of Reason Alone*.[1] He thinks of four principal features as defining the Enlightenment and, therefore, by extension, much of the modern mentality. The first is "*ratiocination* as the organon of the age." Reason had become, in other words, no longer a means of participating in a larger and still rather mysterious reality, but as an instrument to use within and against and over nature. The second is "humanity, somewhat abstractly viewed, [as] its chief concern." The third feature is "historical optimism," the idea that history, as a matter of course, brings improvements and advances in the human condition: the idea of progress, generally experienced and taken as the natural development of things. The fourth feature regards the Enlightenment's "unhistorical" view of humanity and thus its inability to appreciate the historical and cultural conditions of ancient texts such as the Bible.

Now, I want to point out two things. The first is that this is a fairly typical assessment of the Enlightenment period and its intellectual presuppositions. No one pretends that, during this period, all thought alike; nor, of course, do all think alike today. But there are now, as there were then, recognizable thoughts that seemed to work quite well as the common basis of agreement among people who discussed matters of any seriousness concerning the world, humanity, religion, and the like. We still recognize the rhetorical strength of referring with much assurance to "scientific reason," to "human rights," to "progressive" positions in science, politics, theology, or what have you. And we are likely to be as incensed at President Thomas Jefferson for owning slaves as if he had lived after World War II and should have known better.

The second point that I want to make is that each of these marks of modernity is characterized by a spirit of "freedom" from their objects. That is another way of saying that it has to do with the separation or "distraction" from the object.

The first "mark"—reason—is intended to give us general understanding of things, so that we can participate in a world of particulars. The Enlightenment approach does just the opposite; it is rather a means of setting our sights on the uses and behavior of specific things so that we might control them. Its earlier aim was knowledge, and its later aim was power. "The positive force at its core was a determined assertion of the freedom of the individual—freedom in affairs social and political, intellectual and religious."[2] The earlier direction of reason was to take the human mind "higher" into those realms for which reason fits the mind; the new direction is to give it "freedom" from those realms in the sense that it becomes the master of them. To enter into the general consideration of things is a "participatory" power—such as the power of love and contemplation. But to gain mastery over things is always to find oneself strongly separated and, in other words, "distracted" or pulled away, from those things. The modern use of reason was for the sake of that separation, that pulling away, and that freedom that only mastery can provide. It was Bacon, of course, who gave us the modern dictum that so sets the agenda of modernity: "Knowledge is power." And it was Descartes who explained that science is to make us "the masters and possessors of nature." Jürgen Moltmann made a revealing statement about this new sense of the purposes of reason: "Scientific reason is instrumentalizing reason, reason whose epistemological drive is utilization and domination. This pushed out the older receptive reason, which was an organ of perception, and the earlier *phronesis*, which clothed reason in the wisdom of experience. According to Kant's *Critique of Pure Reason*, modern reason only now sees 'what it itself has brought forth according to its own design', by 'compelling nature to give an answer to its questions' (preface to the second edition). *This coercion of nature is called 'experiment', and in the eighteenth century it was often compared with inquisition under torture.*"[3]

The second feature, according to Greene, is "humanity, somewhat abstractly viewed, [as] its chief concern." The idea here is not altogether different from that of reason. It is the human as *subject* that comes into view—the human with a will, who lives a life shaped by the freedom to choose. It is contrary to the more natural disposition, if you consider it in the light of real experience, that the human being *responds* to what is already there. The human being should hope to respond intelligently and morally to a world that was there long before he arrived, which extends beyond his personal experience and seems to demand that he respond purposefully (that is, morally) to the community of persons and things. Yet the human as subject seems to ignore that more customary—and, I would have to say, natural—experience, in favor of the enticements of "being in control."

Kant's famous 1784 essay on the definition of the "Enlightenment" paints the appealing picture of the *emancipated* human being, set free to live in accordance with his or her own reason and will. One is, under these conditions, not subject to the traditions and the history that preceded, but delivered from them. Once again: notice the theme of "separation," though the words are "liberation" and freedom from the "yoke of guardians." The mature citizen no longer needs these guardians: "a book which provides meaning for me, a pastor who has a conscience for me, a doctor who will judge my diet for me and so on."[4] The individual is enjoined to separate himself from things formerly considered normal social support. What one might have considered a benefit that a human being *participates* in is now viewed as bonds that one needs to be severed from, or a yoke that needs to be removed.

Historical optimism, and the idea of the perfectibility of the human being, which is Greene's third point, separates the human being from moral responsibility. The "good" is not something that one must discern and choose: it is an historical process, an inevitability. One might be "progressive" in that he attaches himself to this irresistible stream of history; or one might be "reactionary" or "conservative" in that the stream of history is resisted or resented. But the meaning of life has little to do with his own moral responses to the "good," only with his acquiescence in the "tide of history." In traditional morality, one was called forth to do justice on the basis of the idea of a human being made in the image of God. The individual never fully succeeded in answering that call and was judged by his failure or faithful response. The actions of the person became thereby meaningful in the highest sense and, one might say, in the tragic sense of the high calling of a human being to which one could never on one's own respond adequately. But it is a struggle with profound meaning and significance. This could not be said, increasingly, of the modern person. The good is an *inevitable* and *inexorable* attainment that has little to do with the struggles, the triumphs, or the failures of the person in his own life. In many ways talk of "progressive" ideas, or "lifestyles," or choices—notions that supposedly require "courage," a substitute for "right and wrong"—is the most debilitating and dehumanizing of the marks of modernity. It means little more than that one must join in or be left behind. While its rhetoric is, like that of Kant's, one of freedom and courage, it actually narrows the choices of an individual to the meaningless, renouncing his moral judgment in favor of the impersonal stream of historical progress.

The fourth point should seem quite ironic. Greene says that it is characteristic of the Enlightenment thought to be ahistoric in character: "And because it failed to understand the part played by historical events in shaping the thought of the past, it was equally unsympathetic towards historical influences at work in its own thinking. It failed, in a word, to appreciate the fundamental conception of historical genesis and growth."[5] Even Hume and Kant, says Greene, were not free from this characteristic. It is ironic in that, while much confidence is expressed by modern thinkers in historic "processes"—in other words, in history viewed abstractly—little confidence is expressed in the particulars and the peculiarities of history as it has been experienced. Modern people typically feel perfectly competent to judge the actions and motives of past generations on the basis of their *own* prejudices, and without thought of entering sympathetically into the prejudices of a past generation.

In each of these is embedded a "distraction" of the sort I see as typical of the modern sentiment. The first definition of "distract" from the *Oxford English Dictionary* is "To draw in different directions; to draw asunder or apart; to draw away; to separate, divide." And though this is an antique way of using the word, it also reflects the etymology of the term and the truth of what is at work deep in the modern psyche. Reason and the idea of "humanity as subject" give us a sense of mastery over nature and reality, but also draw us apart from nature and reality, so that we understand ourselves no longer as participants, but as observers and as manipulators. Of course, not to see ourselves as participants in something that is a great deal more inclusive than we are is absurd; but then modernity has never allowed absurdity to completely blunt its ambitions. History as an inexorable process, rather than as the experiences of real men and women in a struggle to understand and respond to the world in which they found themselves, separates the human mind from its proper object in contemplating human experience. Each of these sentiments draws us away from the object of thought or reflection, rather than closer to it. Rather than entering sympathetically into real experience, we tend to operate through these abstract understandings and call them concrete.

I shall never forget the experience, as a teenager, of reading Marx and taking him rather seriously when he spoke of siding with the proletariat. Then, in a footnote, he explains that he doesn't mean by this those truly unfortunate waifs and derelicts on the streets—these he said are the *lumpenproletariat*, and not worth considering in regard to the concrete science of history. It occurred to me that he wasn't really dealing with people, as they are found, certainly not with poor people, or even with workers, but *with ideas of people in the most abstract categories*. This is unfortunately the way Marx and later liberation theologies dealt with what they called the "concrete" realities of history.

Participation

The "distraction" that I have described—and which I have claimed to see at the heart of modernity—is opposed by the idea of "participation." There is a difference, for instance, in the idea of "knowledge" that might be stated this way: we can know something in order to have mastery over it—that is what I call "distraction"; or we can know something in order to participate in the world which we attempt to know. The latter motive for knowing is distinctly human and natural, but it is also not precisely the characteristic *modern* motive.

So, what is meant by "participation"? I often think back to the times that I have climbed the steps up the tower of the *Stiftkirche* in Tübingen, Germany, to what was once the earliest observatory of Johannes Kepler, the astronomer. What were his thoughts in studying the stars and planets with rude seventeenth century instruments? We happen to know something of his apparent thoughts and motives because he left good records of them. And we know that, as a scientist, his motives were distinctly different from those that developed from the Baconian philosophy of science, an interest centered in power and mastery over nature.

At the close of his *Harmonice mundi* (1619), Kepler offers a prayer. "It remains for me," he says, "at the very last, to take my eyes and hands away from the table of proofs, lift them up to heaven, and pray devoutly and humbly to the Father of light." In this prayer, he touches upon a sentiment that seems to pervade the work from the beginning, a work performed out of a sense of vocation, because "Thou hast made me delight in thy handiwork." The enjoyment of nature and the knowledge of it are mutually strengthening experiences. One level of enjoyment and knowledge leads to another higher level, for the "light of Nature" has the purpose of moving in us "the desire for the light of grace, so that by it thou mayest bring us over into the light of glory."[6] The idea that science aids the human mind, and indeed the human life, to enter into the reality of existence is evident in Kepler's expression of his work.

Kepler was a scientific realist, which is to say that he believed it the object of science to move toward an increasingly more faithful representation of reality. Observation and attending to the object of study moves us toward correspondence with reality, not toward construction grounded in the imagination, but rather *using* the imagination as an aid toward an intellectual grasp of an intelligible world. At the same time, to say that representation moves toward reality is not to say that it overtakes it. There remains, and we must believe there always remains, a separation and a tension between the "thing-in-itself" and what we understand of it. The work of understanding therefore is pervaded by a sense of wonder and is approached with profound humility.

It is often forgotten that this sense of wonder, and this attempt to represent things in a spirit akin to prayer, is among the earliest motives for science. In the Greek philosophic tradition, science was closely linked with the need for participation in reality. In the Christian tradition—especially in the Western and Augustinian branch of that tradition, which, after all, proved exceptionally fruitful for the physical sciences—science is linked with love. We know in order to love, and love promotes knowledge. Scholars have often remarked on another source of interest in science that became remarkably evident during the Renaissance and the Enlightenment, that which is more akin to magic and alchemy than to a sense of wonder. It exploits the desire to control and to use things for greedy or selfish purposes. Kepler's early career was marked by his dabbling in astrology, for which he had no real love, but which the academic market of his time tended to promote. One year he predicted a cold winter and the invasion of the Turks into Austria. He was correct on both counts, and received a promotion the next year.

Yet these two motives—the motive to know in order to participate and love, and then the motive to know in order to master and control—were in competition with each other. In reality they still are, since moral choices really never become out of date. But it is the more participatory, rather than the controlling (and what I have called distracting) motive that we need to understand here. And this is where St. Augustine can help us. It was his reflections, very early in this process, that allowed thinking people to understand how our love defines us, and allows us to participate in the world in which we live.

St. Augustine says that we relate to things and to people, as well as to God, in two possible ways. We either use them, or we enjoy them. In most cases we do both: we enjoy what we use and use what we enjoy. That which is lower than we are, however, are the things that we use principally. That which is higher than we are, we are called upon to enjoy principally. In relation to the lowest of things, we use only. In relation to God, the highest of all, we enjoy only. The disorder in life, in our moral life, comes from confusing what and to what extent things are to be used, and what, on the other hand, is to be enjoyed. The Bishop of Hippo even describes this disorder as a kind of "distraction":

> Supposing then we were exiles in a foreign land, and could only live happily in our own country, and that being unhappy in exile we longed to put an end to our unhappiness and return to our own country, we would of course need land vehicles or sea-going vessels, which we would have to make use of in order to be able to reach our own country, where we could find true enjoyment. And then suppose we were delighted with the pleasures of the journey, and with the very experience of being conveyed in carriages or ships, and that we were converted to enjoying what we ought to have been using, and were unwilling to finish the journey quickly, and that by being perversely captivated by such agreeable experiences we lost interest in our own country, where alone we could find real happiness in its agreeable familiarity. Well that's how it is in this mortal life in which we are exiles *away from the Lord* (2 Cor. 5:6); if we wish to return to our home country, where alone we can be truly happy, we have to use this world, not enjoy it, so that we may behold *the invisible things of God, brought to our knowledge through the things that have been made* (Rom. 1:20); that is, so that we may proceed from temporal and bodily things to grasp those that are eternal and spiritual.[7]

To attempt to use God is blasphemous, and it is at the heart of the "quid pro quo" type of religion, in which I do something or other on this level of life in order to gain the cooperation of God in achieving what I want. That is using God. On the other hand, to attempt to enjoy food too much, when in fact it should be mainly used, is cause for the vice of gluttony. And to use a friend, when he ought mainly to be enjoyed, and used only to the extent that he helps us on our way toward God, is a sin against love of neighbor.

At any rate, here you can get the picture. Disorder comes from confusing the need to use and the need to enjoy. Both are intended to lead us on our way toward God. But if we use what we should enjoy it rather distracts us from that supreme aim. And if we enjoy what we ought to use, we are likewise distracted. So the ordered life, one that is as free as possible from these distractions is one that always has in view the aim of life (as the Shorter Catechism puts it, "To love God and to enjoy Him forever") and thus appropriately uses what ought to be used and in the way it ought to be used, and also enjoys what ought to be enjoyed and in a way appropriate to its nature. The aim of knowing anything, for Augustine, is pricisely this, to know how and for what reason we might relate to it. This, as one can see, is the kind of knowledge aimed at participation.

The place and the power of "attention"

To live as a human being is to live with a certain awareness of *vocatio,* of vocation, of being called into life for a purpose. It is, to a greater or lesser degree, to become aware of being caught up in seeking that purpose whether as an individual or in connection with a group, a family, a nation, a profession. The response to just such a sense of vocation gives rise to art, manners, custom, laws, and the innumerable ways, means and modes of life together. A culture, moreover, that is life-giving and humane, peaceable and kind, productive of beauty in music and art, and one that promotes health in body and mind, is a culture that arises out of attention: attentiveness, that is, to that into which, with which, and for the sake of which we are called. Culture of the humane and life-giving sort arises from attention to the nature of things and people and to our relationship to them. "Extreme attention," said Simone Weil, "is what constitutes the creative faculty in man and the only extreme attention is religious. The amount of creative genius in any period is strictly in proportion to the amount of extreme attention, and thus of authentic religion, at that period." For her, prayer and culture inevitably go together. "Attention, taken to its highest degree, is the same thing as prayer."[8]

To be a modern person, I have argued, largely means to be distracted. Distraction is in the design of modernity. To the extent that we singly or in groups are occasionally and even inevitably drawn back into attending to the question of why we are here makes us merely, or one should say truly, human. It is what we have in common with all human beings at all times. And we, as they all do, draw from whatever resources we have at hand, present and past. It is not an especially modern task, in the sense that it attends to what is "just now" (*modo*), but neither is it less a task appropriate for today than for any day. To the extent, however, that we have covenanted together as a society—as a culture of sorts—to be distracted from that task is to be *modern* in the way we have learned over the past three centuries to use the term. It is to agree that though the world and its meaning are unknowable, the world is not unusable. Thus we are drawn to its uses and drawn away from its meaning, its purpose, and even its true enjoyment.

To attend to something is to contemplate it along with its purpose, its highest good, its *telos*. Attending to a person means the same thing. It is to consider the person in his or her own concreteness—including circumstances, personality, habits, suffering, hopes, limitations—along with that person's highest purpose. This is not totally a consideration of the particularities of a person. Nor is it totally an idealistic vision, or an eschatological vision, of who that person might be. But it is considering one in the light of the other. It does not mean, necessarily, that we understand the concrete reality in any profound way, nor that we understand the *telos*. But it is the willingness to hold the two thoughts together, knowing that without both we cannot even approximate, or take two steps in the direction of, understanding a person or even a thing that God has created.

If I am speaking with a man who lives in squalid conditions on the streets of Waco and consider only his present condition, I have not fully come to attend to who this person is in reality. For only when I hold alongside the meager understanding I have of his present condition the high purpose to which he has been called, and the nobility for which he was created, do I recognize the full tragedy of his present condition. Or if I have an ideal and rather abstract picture of "the human being" which guides me in my relationship to a person, and fail to attend to his rotten clothes, and his disorderly habits, and where he must sleep at night, then I have understood him even less. That is why "attending" involves me in both: that which it means to live in the promised and anticipated image of God, and that which is the concrete reality of the moment. One vision alone is idealism; the other is materialism. Both together evokes tragedy in the pagan soul of an honest pagan, and it evokes hope in those who have believed that even the dead, let alone the poor and destitute, are subject to the Spirit of redemption and resurrection.

Simone Weil said that attention is the same as prayer. Let's try to understand what that means. Suppose we pray for someone who is desperately ill. In attending to that person, in holding this person before our minds eye and in the presence of God, we necessarily have in view the condition that we find him in at the moment. We also, at the same time, bring to mind his healing and his restoration. At one and the same time we take seriously the patient's illness and we take equally seriously his restored health. It is not possible to pray for someone's healing without doing both. That is attending.

What I have wished to make plain in these pages is that modernity wishes to pull apart (distract) what, in the eyes of faith, belong together. The opposite of this disorder is attention. I am necessarily recalled to the days when I first went out on the church field and found myself in association with other ministers. Among them always were those who, with simple faith and sometimes not much education, saw the world in what I believed was a naïve and inadequate way. I was in Georgia; and these were the "wool-hatted" fundamentalist preachers for whom Flannery O'Conner had so much fondness and felt, in ways only she could express, a certain kinship. Yet often their analysis of the world, this secular world-age, was that it was dying of "prayerlessness." I think Flannery O'Conner would agree. I know Simone Weil would agree. And now, after many more years of a different kind of education, I find that I must also agree. They were right all along.

— 6 —

Power

*What is happiness?—The feeling that power increases—
that a resistance is overcome.*

Friedrich Nietzche, *The Anti-Christ*

*The kings of the Gentiles lord it over them; and those
in authority are called benefactors. But not so with you;
rather the greatest among you must become like the
youngest, and the leader like one who serves.*

Jesus, the Christ[1]

I F THE PROPER TASK of the humane community is its quest for
meaning, purpose, truth, love, beauty, justice, and all of those
qualities that enrich the life together and add to the dignity of
each member of society, then whatever opposes that quest—or opposes the very spirit of such a quest—also opposes the very idea of
community. That seems to me clear enough.

68

The point I have attempted to make, however, is that such op-position almost inevitably comes indirectly, in the form of a distraction. We do not deny our human dignity, or the sort of notion about humanity that might be associated with a doctrine of the *imago dei*, but we are distracted from it: we are distracted from attending to the ends and attend instead to the means. This should become very evident as we examine the shape of modernity; for in modern times we are possessed of very powerful *means*, and it is a powerful temptation to think that our *end* is but the *means*. This is, of course, Allen Tate's definition of secularism: when the means of a society are seen as its ends.

In this chapter, I want to show how the very idea of power has become a distraction and therefore a hindrance in the cultivating of genuine communities that nourish the human spirit. To do that, I want for us to think about the issue in connection with two thinkers of the early modern period who have had enormous influence upon our civilization and who have, in effect, taught us a certain reverence for power. They are Francis Bacon, who influenced our modern idea of science, and Jean Bodin who had a similar influence upon our notions of political power. In a previous book, *The Long Truce*, I attempted to show how the modern idea of toleration became a justification for that distraction; here I want to say something about the nature of the distraction itself.

Love and Power

I believe it would be helpful, first, to clarify something about the relationship between love and power. Henri Bergson, in his classic work *The Two Sources of Morality and Religion*, demonstrates the unequal necessity of two forces in a living human culture. One of these "forces" is that of obligation, the other is love. New and broader horizons of life are instituted by love. A great irruption of affection in society—usually eminating from only a few charismatic figures, or only from one on occasion—draws many into community. By this enthusiastic spirit of love the life of a people is transformed and new institutions are born, manners and good works reflecting the nature of this new sentiment become widespread and habitual. But just as they become habitual they begin to draw upon something other than love, something other than that irruption of an enthusiasm that compels only in that it draws and attracts according to the voluntary nature of love. This other force he calls "obligation." The institutions, the manners, as well as the disciplines, the attachments, and the structures that had the breath of life breathed into them by love, now begin to operate by the sense of a thousand expectations, laws, rules, and habits pressing upon members of a society, causing them to conform to a pattern of life and conversation whether or not they will to do so. And though there will be some who resist, and some who try to conform unsuccessfully, nevertheless social life is enlarged and elevated and made to pattern itself in such a way that it serves the interest of those higher faculties of human beings and together they express a nobility and a greater longing for goodness, beauty, and justice. This is the lasting imprint of love—lasting but never permanent, of course, in a life that always sees the contests of these higher aspirations and these lower urges.

Three points are to be stressed here.

First, in no human and earthly society is it possible to live with only one of these, either the life-breathing enthusiasm of love, or the institutionalizing and organizing force of obligation. Love dissipates without the institution; and the institution sustains the occasion and the opportunity for love. This was the point in Dietrich Bonhoeffer's famous "Wedding Sermon from Prison," to the effect that it is marriage that sustains love and not love that sustains marriage. However, the other side is that the institution cannot substitute for love, and the organized form can become, and often does become, deadly to the living spirit.

Second, at the same time we must bear in mind that they are *contrary forces*, and they work upon us not only in different ways but in opposite ways. Obligation works upon us—like law—through our propensity to fear. Thus we tend to be law-abiding; thus we tend on average to obey rules—society would become unbearable without this tendency. Love operates, however, through the heightened passions, the desire for what is the object of love. "Perfect love drives out fear," said the Apostle John.[2] Through love the person is not driven but drives, for love has no need of rules; it has outstripped obligation already. This is why poets such as Marion Montgomery and Andrew Lytle have insisted that the opposite of love is not hate but power. They are opposing principles, even though in this world neither can be left behind.

Third, the last point, which takes us directly to the crisis of modern life that we are addressing is this: since power (in terms of obligation, law, coercion, rule, organization) imitates the works of love, and indeed has a role in giving them a "place" in which to work, we are tempted to think it is a worthy substitute for love. It has the further advantage of not having to appeal to the affections and the will of members of society. It short-circuits the cultivation of the human spirit, and compels instead the cooperation of people through the agency (at one level or another) of fear.

With these distinctions in mind, I would like now to follow with two early modern, and very formative, influences upon the way we view the use of power.

Jean Bodin (1529/30-1596)

My earlier study of the modern idea of "toleration" turned up an interesting pattern of thought among its early proponents. Of the earliest *modern* thinkers who formulated a theory of toleration, all favored strengthening the central government. There is a certain irony in this. On the one hand, regarding religion, they worked to diminish the established authority—the authority of the church. On the other hand, regarding government, they favored increasing and strengthening the established authority. This was true, in different ways, of Jean Bodin, John Locke, Pierre Bayle, and John Stuart Mill. It is important to remember that the church represented the most potent of the various non-governmental authorities in society, but it was only one of them. As Bertrand de Jouvenal points out, on numerous occasions, but especially in his book *On Power*, every social group or association develops its own sense of authority, discovers its own vocation, and its own power structure, simply by virtue of its being a group. Therefore, besides individuals at one end of the societal spectrum, and central governments at the other end, there are numerous associations which enjoy some influence and exercise some authority in the life of the individual and of the larger community. That is true of the family, the guild, the neighborhood or region, the ethnic group, and the religious association or church. To a greater or lesser degree, these authorities compete with one another and limit one another. Therefore they represent, each in a greater or lesser way, an authority that limits the government. Since powers normally wish to increase, they tend to resent anything that limits them. None competes with governmental power so effectively as does the authority of religion.

Therefore, the first line of resistance to government authority will naturally be the authority of the church. And it was the first to put difficulties in the path of a more comprehensive development of government such as we find with the early modern emergence of the nation-state.

The realization of this conflict was occasioned by a crisis in authority. The church, which had been the framework for European society for hundreds of years, was now no longer united. In dividing, the church precipitated political divisions as well. The religious wars of the sixteenth and seventeenth century were a part of this readjustment of powers. They were the occasion, also, for the growth in scope and power of the civil authorities and the centralized sovereignty in England, France, Spain, Scotland, Muscovy, and Sweden, foreshadowing, of course, other developments at a later time in Germany, Italy and elsewhere.

We are offered, in the life of Jean Bodin, and in his considerable contribution to the intellectual life of his times, something of a prism through which to view the very changes that we have been discussing all along. For here is a man with deep roots in medieval European thought. He is nevertheless one who, like many of his day caught up in the religious and civil disturbances of their time, was stimulated to think through to the first principles involved in understanding religion, on the one hand, and in understanding the fundamentals of civic life on the other.

Bodin argued for absolute sovereign authority in the state, rather than the shared authority of multiple associations. It is often assumed, and with good reason, that he was strongly influenced by Machiavelli.[3] And in religion, he was convinced that the truth of religion lies in the general principles behind the particulars found in the variety of public religions. The former theory he explored and expounded especially in his *Six Books of the Commonwealth*, on which most of his reputation is built. The latter theory was the product of the time after he was no longer actively in public life and was published as the *Heptaplamares* only after his death. But the two theories—one of political authority and the other of religious toleration—undoubtedly belong together.

When one considers the need for order within a commonwealth, religion is bound to introduce controversy and imbalance. It is well known that religion sometimes gives rise to zealotry, and the magistrate must respond accordingly. "The lunatic who cannot stop dancing and singing incessantly," Bodin writes, "cannot be calmed unless the musician first attunes his violin to the patient's mood, and then gradually modifies the rhythm till he has cured him." This argument might well conclude that the magistrate should impose religion. Bodin noted that the world had seen "the kingdoms of Sweden, Scotland, Denmark, and England, the Swiss Confederates and the Empire of Germany all change their religion, though the commonwealth preserved its republican or monarchical form unaltered in each case."[4] His principle point, however, is that the issue of temporal order ought to take precedence over religious questions. "All questions which are made matters of debate," he says, "become thereby matters of doubt . . . . But it is a great impiety to make a matter of doubt of the thing which each man should be certain about and hold to resolutely . . . . If philosophers and mathematicians do not question the principles of their sciences, why should one be permitted to question a religion which has once been accepted and approved . . . It is well known that the kings of the East and of Africa strictly forbid any discussion of religion." In Spain and Muscovy, he says further, the authorities "forbad preaching, or even discussion of religion on pain of death."[5]

Bodin was the first to suggest that the business of the expanding European commonwealths was not to determine how governments might contribute to the public good, but to public order and wealth. He readily admitted that the law of God was a higher law than the law of the magistrate. In this he was no innovator. What was new, in Bodin, was the willingness to separate the two, making the law of God no longer strictly relevant to the keeping of public order. That he was irresolute in this move toward the privitizing of religion is clear. Locke would finally make the break and bring to fruition what Bodin had only intimated. For now, he "could neither say consistently with the schoolmen, let us consider things as they ought to be if the purposes of God are to be accomplished, or with Machiavelli, let us consider things as they must be if men are to have what they desire."[6] Nevertheless, Bodin clearly marks a new path in political thought, that power itself (heretofore thought of as a means), along with wealth, had become the "ends" toward which the art of politics aims.

Details regarding the religious thought of Jean Bodin are sketchy and have given rise to interesting speculation. It is probable that his father was a tailor, and though not of the nobility, he was securely in the rising bourgeoisie and was able to afford dowries for his four daughters and a financial legacy for his three sons. For years, the story persists that Jean's mother was Jewish. Evidence, according to most students of Bodin and his period, seems to contradict this notion; still, there are those who point to the fact that Jean Bodin's enrollment in a Carmelite house may even argue for his Jewish genealogy. In Spain of that time, though this fact is not conclusive in regard to France, only the Carmelites and the Jesuits would admit those who had Jewish ancestry. Nevertheless, the argument for the Jewish mother of Bodin is primarily of this negative sort, except for the fact that, for some reason, he shows throughout his life an enormous interest in pursuing fundamental questions about the truth of religion.

As a youth, Bodin was sent to Paris, a city that for three hundred years had been the center of European learning. Once again, he was enrolled in a Carmelite house. During his time there, when he would have been nineteen or twenty, an incident occurred that caused an uproar in Paris and an intense disturbance throughout the region. The setting for the incident was the spirit of religious reform that had swept Europe and caused a disruption in the church and in national politics for three decades. The effects in France had become especially pronounced since the publication of Calvin's *Institutes* in 1536, a mere dozen years before three Carmelite brothers were called before the Parliament of Paris charged with heresy. Among these brothers was one Jean Bodin. Was this the same as our Bodin, later a political theorist of international fame, or was he another? We do know that whereas two of the alleged heretics were sentenced to death, the one named Bodin was released thanks to the intervention of the bishop of Angers. And it was to this same bishop, Gabriel Bouvery, that Bodin dedicated his 1555 translation of Oppian's *De venatione*. When we couple this fact with the appearance of a Jean Bodin in Geneva, and the marriage of this Bodin to Typhaine Reynaude, the widow of Leonard Gallimard, one of the alleged heretics of the 1548 incident, then we might well suspect that our Bodin had indeed become, or at least flirted with the idea of becoming, a Calvinist. Besides these indications, we know that the Geneva registry shows this name as "Jean Bodin of Saint-Amand," and it so happens that after 1576, the famous author was frequently identified as "of Saint-Amand."

The Carmelite education, the possibility of being swept up in the new spirit of reform in France, the provocative circumstances of being brought up in the home of a woman who was Jewish by birth, and the mere fact of being a denizen of sixteenth-century France is enough to explain Bodin's intense and even scholarly interest in religion. But there is also the fact that this Bodin could not have long been found in Geneva, since he was shortly back in France, claiming to be a Catholic and giving evidence of leaning toward tolerationist views with regard to religious differences. It is well to remember that the burning of Michel Servetus, the socinian heretic, took place in Geneva with the approval of John Calvin in 1553. This could well explain the return of Bodin to France and to the Catholic fold. And this incident, together with the narrow escape before the Parliament of Paris, may well explain his later sympathy for policies of religious toleration.

His views of religion were not, of course, fixed throughout his life. They changed to such an extent that one early interpreter said, "About the religion of the man nothing can be said more certain than that his religion varied with the various years of his life."[7] Yet there was a certain consistency, or at least a detectable trajectory, that reveals something of his mature religious thought. He was influenced by the Platonism that prevailed in sixteenth-century Paris. For him, the particulars and the variety of life could be understood by plumbing to the level of unity and harmony. It is true of nature; it is also true of religions. This is a vision of life that takes on greater importance in the years of French conflagration and civil unrest due to religious disputes.

The late sixties through the seventies were particularly restless years for Bodin personally and for his countrymen. The maelstrom of religious claims and counterclaims was rising, creating havoc in the political realm. An effort to settle the issue on the side of the Catholic interests resulted in a 1568 edict against those of the Reformed faith, dismissing all Protestants from government positions and requiring oaths of loyalty to the Catholic faith by members of the parliaments and the university faculties.

Bodin came under suspicion. In 1569 and 1570 he was imprisoned for a year and a half, accused of being an adherent of the "new religion." After his release he was appointed counselor to Francis, the duke of Alençon. Francis was a leader of the *Politiques*. As a bourgeois political movement, the *Politiques* favored religious toleration and civil neutrality in the dispute between Protestants and Catholics. At the same time they did not favor resistance to the monarchy based upon religious convictions. The fact that they favored religious toleration, however, meant that they shared with the minority Protestants in France an important point in their political agenda. So the move from a level of Protestant conviction (and no one knows precisely how convinced Bodin might have been) to the circles of the *Politiques* seems more than plausible.

Bodin found himself at the center of these struggles. Alençon was a pretender to the throne of France, but was outmaneuvered by Henry III. In spite of Bodin's connections with the leader of the *Politiques*, he evidently found favor in the new king's court and attempted to influence the regime in the direction of policies favored by the *Politiques*. In 1581, he accompanied Alençon, whose intentions were to court Queen Elizabeth, on his second journey to England. There he became well known to the Queen of England and to Secretary Walsingham. It was on this occasion that we find Bodin making the case against the persecution of Catholics by the Protestant English regime. Perhaps it is here that we can speculate he moved from Protestant sympathies to tolerationist views, if not clearly to Catholicism. In response to the hanging of Edmund Campion in 1581, he writes to the Queen and her court, that "if the prince [is] well assured of the truth of his religion would draw his subjects thereunto, divided into sects and factions, he must not, therein, use force." His argument foreshadows views later taken up by himself in writings not published until after his death, and indeed it foreshadows views not seen clearly again until the time of Pierre Bayle and John Locke: "For that the minds of men, the more they are forced, the more forward and stubborn they are, and the greater punishment that shall be inflicted upon them the less good is to be done, the nature of man being commonly such as may of it selfe bee led to like of anything, but never enforced so to do."[8]

We might imagine that, with the world and especially France erupting in conflicts, intrigues, treachery, assassinations, and in "wars and the rumor of war," men's minds were easily turned to consider the source of such unaccountable troubles. Like people of other ages they turned to the possibility that the source of such problems was not the visible world but the invisible one, a world of angels and demons which alone seemed capable of explaining the fiendish nature of the events that swirled around them. Bodin found himself in the midst of the witch-hunting fever that—contrary to the modern propoganda concerning medieval times—did not so much characterize the middle ages as it did the early modern period. It was the age of Bacon, Newton, and Hobbes that was obsessed with the idea of witches and demons, not the age of Aquinas and Duns Scotus. In 1578, Jean Bodin presided at the witch trial of Joanna Harvilleria. She was convicted and condemned to burn at the stake as was the custom for witches during the early days of the Enlightenment, both in Europe and in New England.

One is tempted to speculate as to why there should be such an outbreak of interest in the demonic and in sorcery at this particular time. Was there anything to the matter other than the obvious excitement over so many insurmountable problems? Certainly the theories of René Girard give us some leads. It is impossible to understand human violence and the part it plays in civilization, he would argue, without facing forthrightly what happens when society is confronted with overwhelming problems. In the midst of plagues, economic collapse, civil war, and other problems that seem both inexplicable and insoluble, people often resort to "magical thinking." In other words they resort to the belief that there is a solution to a problem that seems otherwise to have no solution, that the solution is on the level of possible action, and that someone is responsible for the great misfortunes that seem so impenetrable. Quoting the ethnologist E. E. Evans-Pritchard he says that magical thought seeks "a significant cause on the level of social relations."[9] The magical solution to the problem comes to be "in other words a human being, a victim, a scapegoat."[10]

We must join this insight of Girard's, however, with that of Jürgen Moltmann and others concerning a central obsession of the dawning modern age. It was an obsession with power. Bacon's idea that knowledge is power, and Descartes' notion that science exists for the sake of making us the "masters and possessors of nature," are at this time becoming a new pattern of thought. Power has become the centerpiece of a new kind of harmony, one based no longer on the "right relation of things" in a world that both begins and ends in mystery, but it is a harmony that comes from control. That anyone thought that such control was possible was a modern idea. And when science seemed very much like magic, the temptation was to be swept along by anything that offered the same promise of control. It was especially tempting in an age that seemed so out of control.

In just such an atmosphere Bodin wrote his 1580 work, *De la démonomanie des sorciers*. It was produced on the heels of his famous trial and condemnation of the unfortunate Joanna Harvilleria. How can the thoughtful, philosophically astute, Bodin have become a principle agent in the furtherance of such practices as the burning of witches? From this distance, we often pretend to be shocked by the violence of the sixteenth century. The truth of the matter, however, is that they would be shocked by ours, if they had known of it. And in this connection, having to do with the burning of witches, we who have lived in the twentieth and twenty-first centuries often project such practices back into medieval times. I have frequently run into references, even by the well educated, to the medieval practice of "witch-burning." But of course it was not medieval, but more distinctively modern. In the sixteenth and seventeenth centuries, there was a virtual craze of witch-hunting throughout most of Europe. Like other modern preoccupations, it seems to have arisen along with the desire to "control" a world that had become both vast and threatening in the wake of new discoveries and new opportunities. In New England, the Puritans were driving people with bribes and the threat of torture to sign the "Devil's Book," thus implicating them in the witchcraft that made them perfect scapegoats for community misfortunes. Including the Salem, Massachusetts, "hysteria" of 1692, there was a rash of witch trials in New England involving over a hundred accusations and after which at least forty defendants were put to death. All this took place, not in medieval Europe, but in America on the verge of the eighteenth century, and in a section of America populated by folk who immigrated from the most industrial parts of England and Holland.

For many this will seem to be a great paradox—modern people with a witch-hunting mentality. Yet perhaps the answer to the paradox is seen in the intellectual disposition of one such as Jean Bodin, whose answer to the knottier problems of theological discourse is to resort to power—to cut the Gordian knot with the sword of the state. Such is not contrary to modernity, but is largely characteristic of it. Having given up on the theological questions and moral questions in the public arena, having consigned them to the sphere of the private, we must eventually deal with our dilemmas, and we do so by the use of power and by the ancient habit of scapegoating—even though, as René Girard has pointed out, the scapegoating now uses all its wiles to hide its true nature.[11]

Francis Bacon (1561-1626)

The son born to Nicolas Bacon, the Lord Keeper of the Great Seal in the court of Elizabeth i, and to Anne Cooke, a puritan Calvinist of noble birth, has been both blamed and praised for his part in giving shape to modern thought. Having been reared in the shadow of the court, and having risen to prominence as a member of Parliament and later holding the office of Lord Chancellor, he was in a position to influence public life and thought. And, for a public figure of some prominence, his philosophical production is truly impressive. But it was work done under enormous burdens of public and private obligations. His interpreter, F. H. Anderson, said, "The crown of his ambition was the direction from a great place with magnificence and magnanimity of widespread and expensive scientific operations. Little of this desire was satisfied. He could obtain neither a college nor a royal foundation, nor even a patron, and the scientific work which he initiated lapsed for a generation after his death. He sought wealth and died in debt, always to be pursued by creditors, and never to use his income to pay assistants for the collecting of the scientific data upon which his new sort of learning was to depend."[12]

The literary production for which he became best known, and which was his chief ambition, was performed in the midst of great political demands occasioned by "intrigues for place" and "the compiling of manifestoes for James and his advisors." Thus, "the majority of his reflections on human learning were set down in intervals between sessions of Parliament, court-sittings, connivings for place, and advices to the King and the King's favorites." As a result, these works, as extensive as they are, "remain tentative in statement, inconclusive in structure, and fragmentary in detail."[13] In the midst of this, he was accused of taking a bribe and was convicted, losing his office of Lord Chancellor. To this day those who wish to make of him a saint in the halls of modern science are at pains to defend him from the charge.

Loren Eiseley writes, in a curious passage, of the "mythology" of this charge that lives on:

> The men of violence have been forgiven. A romantic halo en-
> velops them. But the man who outlived the violence and who
> husbanded his power of survival in order to communicate a great
> secret, our age finds it oddly difficult to forgive. One wonders
> why. Perhaps it is because he was truly a stranger in his own
> age—a civilized man out of his time and place, dealing with
> barbarians and barely evading the rack and gallows in the pro-
> cess. It affronts our sense of dignity to see him bowing painfully
> to titled fools and rapacious upstarts, while presenting books
> hopefully to learned men who scornfully fling them aside. He
> walks hesitantly toward us through history as though he could
> see our century but not reach it; he is out of place.[14]

This passage was written in the early 1960s, perhaps at the peak of that time in the twentieth century when many in the West, and especially in America, held as an article of faith that history brings constant and inevitable improvement. That some things had improved (like technology and medicine) while others had declined (likes mor-als, manners, philosophy, and art) occurred only to a reflective few. So, by the magic of this "historical optimism" that had become a part of the canon of modernity, Loren Eiseley parleyed a simple political bribe into The Man Who Saw Through Time, and lived well ahead of it. Yet it is quite true that Francis Bacon was beginning to think in a way that would become common to people of modern Europe, and would profoundly influence the way we, in our own day, articulate our sense of the world.

The project that he had given himself, and that was announced as "The Great Instauration," was to consist of six parts: a new clas-sification of the sciences; a treatment of the new inductive method; natural history; tables illustrating and classifying the discoveries made by the method of induction; ground-rules for experimentation; and "a philosophical synthesis based upon the tables inductively established."[15] These six parts were never completed; and the work that he did produce represented only part of it, some of those parts being only sketchy representations of what he had projected. However, his eloquent portrayal of the method and purpose of science was to have lasting influence, not his systematic gathering and representation of encyclopedic knowledge. It is this method, and its philosophical justification, that helps us to understand the modern age and its self-consciousness. Of those works he did produce, among the more important are *Novum organum sive indicia de interpretatione naturae* ("The New Organon or True Directions concerning the Interpretation of Nature") which was published in 1620, and *De dignitate et augmentis scientiarum* ("Of the Dignity and Advancement of Learning"), published in 1623.

What is most remarkable about this "Great Instauration"—this renewal or refreshment of the sciences and learning—is its ready dismissal of the progress in learning up to this point in history, and its inauguration of a new plan based upon the powers supposedly locked away in the primitive state of things, which have now been distorted or lost due to the corrupting influence of a tradition of learning. It is a bold desire indeed to want to undo past philosophies and start all over again, but if there is any central effect in Bacon's philosophical rhetoric it was this. Thanks largely to him, the notion of starting again from the beginning, and of doing something "novel," began to be thought a wise, rather than a foolhardy, thing to do. It was not simply an "adding to" that he wanted to accomplish, but a "tearing down" based upon something of a total critique of culture and learning.[16]

There are numerous examples of this approach in Bacon's writings. Indeed, it is impossible to understand Bacon's approach at all without seeing this as his central motive. For instance, in an "Introductory Narrative" to his address on "The Refutation of Philosophies," Bacon writes, "I am preparing a refutation of philosophies but know not how to begin. The road which lies open for others is closed to me. The hosts of errors are so many and so great that it is impossible to engage them singly. They must be overthrown and swept away in masses."[17] One cannot simply bring new insights into the treasury of human knowledge gained by the work of previous generations of thinkers, but Bacon finds it necessary to work "with a view to undermining their authority."

There is a strange irony in this approach. While wishing to undermine the authority of past philosophies, there is a certain veneration for the ancient and, in fact, primitive state of human learning. He complains only that philosophy of contemporary learning has been reduced to a few philosophers such as Plato and Aristotle, who stress the theoretical knowledge, a knowledge that bears little fruit in terms of practical works. A wider inclusion of the ancients would discover the virtues of the arts that create and augment culture. What has happened in the following of philosophy is that "the theoretical sciences, like statues of the gods, are thronged with worshippers, but never move." So, it should be noted that "mechanical arts and philosophy should differ in this way": "In the former the wits of individuals mingle, in the latter they corrupt and destroy one another."[18]

We must pay attention to a certain modesty involved in attempting to add, incrementally, to the body of knowledge. One cannot change everything in that way, only augment what is already there. If, however, you can manage the hubris to believe that you should establish the whole program of learning, then you must begin at the beginning, back with the most ancient of philosophers. There—at the beginnings, in the most primitive stages—you have real power. For it is there, one would think, that the larger agenda and the most basic directions are set. This is where Bacon proposed to place himself, not as an inheritor of Plato and Aristotle, or as one who could contribute his modest insights to time-honored insights of others, but as one who stood side by side with the earliest thinkers. He proposed to start all over again.

This primitivism of certain Enlightenment thinkers reminds us of the movement in philosophy and literature known as Romanticism. From the late eighteenth century to the mid-nineteenth century this sentiment flourished, but in many ways it is a permanent part of modern thought and an always present option. Romanticism, with its tacit rejection of ideas embodying order, balance, harmony, and reason is often thought to be a reaction against the Enlightenment. It is, in fact, a rejection of the Classical side of the Enlightenment, but insofar as it celebrates nature and primitivism, over against civilization and the cultivated attainments of the human being as thinker, artist, builder and planter, it figures prominently in the agenda of the Enlightenment. For in appealing to the primitive state of things, one is also rejecting the refinements of civilization, including the institutions, doctrines, practices, arts, and the traditions in learning and culture that make of society more than a collection of individuals or a crowd living in some proximity, but a finely tuned communal instrument that reflects something of the harmony for which human beings long, becoming a place and a people that nourish the soul and stimulate the noblest aspirations.

But that loss is hardly the focus of Enlightenment thinking. Instead, the thought of beginning again gives the intellectual and the activist a place to stand outside of present existence. It is the stuff of which utopian visions are made, so we should not be surprised that early modern times was productive of a number of famous utopian visions, and that Francis Bacon created one of these in his *New Atlantis*, published sometime after his death. The futuristic and forward-looking scheme of the Enlightenment thinker is somewhat deceptive. It is just as well to stand among the fathers and mothers of the race, for the whole point is to invent something new and to change the world from the ground up. In an uncompleted work, written very early and never published in his lifetime, *De intepretatione naturae prooemium*, Bacon said, "Now I have discovered that nothing is of such benefit to the human race as the discovery of and devotion to new truths and arts by which the life of men is cultivated."[19] The influence and the power to effect something remarkable is paramount; for the Enlightenment period was not simply a period of uncertainty and dangers as some have liked to emphasize,[20] but a time of heady opportunity. New opportunities for trade, including the slave trade that was making some immensely wealthy, and consequently the opportunities for the organization of the state on a vast scale also had their impact. It was easy for some to imagine that one could make the world all over again, "sweeping away everything else in masses."

A comparable impulse is found in Descartes, whose *Meditations* documents an attempt to take oneself out of the middle of existence and find a place to stand outside of tradition or the environment of nature, finding instead the point at which one knows that one thinks, and then rebuilds knowledge of the world from that isolated point. One cannot help being reminded of Archimedes who said, "Give me a place to stand and I will move the earth."[21] The Enlightenment thinker's dream, and it is a fantastic dream that has much colored our world, is to find that place, sometimes among the primitives, in order to move or to make the world all over again. The issue is not so much epistemology as it is power.

We find something very similar in John Locke's "defense" of the Christian faith in *The Reasonableness of Christianity* (1695). This work is an attempt to say that the founding documents of Christianity, the New Testament and some amount of background from the Old Testament, are quite enough to establish the "reasonableness of Christianity" and that the innovations that have taken place through the intervening years in the ecumenical councils and among divines is just so much "wrangling" that has served to complicate what is essentially a simple thing. Locke plows through the scriptures in a most tedious way and, as Eric Voegelin points out, with "meager results." But from Locke's point of view, those meager results are all that is required—to believe that Jesus is the Messiah and, on that basis, to follow his teachings. Of course, in his meticulous treatment of scripture passages, Locke comes right up to the brink of having to deal with problems that theologians found themselves faced with when *they* took seriously the disclosures of Scripture. The result for the theologians of the church, of course, was the unfolding of certain theological lines of thought that proved to be guidelines for the church in knowing the further implications of the scripture.

But this is precisely what Locke wanted to avoid. So each time he found himself confronted with issues that might quickly turn into theological issues, he withdrew. All along he would make the point that these silly speculations were not really needed, that what was needed was clear in Scripture, and that was good, reasonable, and clear enough.

The underlying theme, then, was not the virtues of Christianity so much as the vice of every theological refinement that has occurred since Scripture was written. Locke's understanding of Christianity from his earliest days as a writer on such subjects was that the development of the priesthood and orthodoxy was a way of manipulating the populace to be influenced by the church and to prevent the domination of proper governmental authorities. As Robert Kraynak has put it, "this ethical religion of Jesus was soon transformed into a priestly religion of authoritative dogma and worship. Ambitious clerics introduced doctrines and creeds, and prescribed forms of worship in order to make salvation dependent upon belief in abstruse dogma and performance of elaborate ceremonies; and they establish church government to enforce their prescriptions against those who dissented. In other words, a priestly class made itself indispensable to the people by arrogating to itself exclusive powers from God."[22]

The unstated premise of *The Reasonableness of Christianity*, therefore, is that Christian people can well do without all the refinement and theologizing that has taken place over the earlier seventeen centuries, that all that is truly needed is the Bible, and that the Bible can be understood by any unprejudiced mind without the help of priests and the "writers and wranglers" of religion. Such an approach caused Eric Voegelin to comment that Locke interpreted the Bible as if it were a book written yesterday, and that when he wrote of Christian thought he made a *tabula rasa* of seventeen centuries of Western culture. Attempting to make such a point as Locke was making, of course, undergirds Locke's other point about toleration. For in his contention for religious toleration he argues that religion properly belongs to the sphere of the private life and must be removed from the realm of public decisions about public matters. This separation of the public and the private, and the confinement as far as possible of the religious life to the private, is naturally augmented by this understanding of the adequacy of the Bible alone without the accretion of generations of theological development. In other words, it aided his programmatic separation of religion from the public sphere if such refinements as theologians bring to biblical knowledge were, in fact, unnecessary to the faith.

What is the motivation, however, behind such an argument? Why is returning to the most primitive expression of Christianity better than that which, over the centuries, includes the further reflection of the church upon the fuller meaning of the gospel? The benefit could be, of course, that if the tradition—whether the intellectual traditions of divines or the tradition of worship and practice refined over time in the church—has strayed far from the original intent of the founders of Christianity, then there still exists a canon—which in fact is a part of that tradition—that serves as a touchstone by which the later tradition itself could be remedied. But that benefit is retained only if the later tradition as well as the scriptures are valued—the one serving as an amplification of the other, while the other serves as an anchor to the whole process, and both together making the gospel available to multiple ages of hearers and believers. This was the point of view of the Protestant Reformers with their doctrine of *sola scriptura*—but it was not John Locke's intention, nor the intention of the typical founder of Enlightenment thinking. Instead, Locke's obvious intention was to make religion a matter for which the private citizen is competent, so that theological judgments could be erased from the public agenda, which was now to be governed by "rational" purposes. Rational, in this case, means that which serves the purposes of material existence and the secular agenda of public agencies and commercial enterprises. His purpose was not to reserve for Scripture the power to "correct" tradition, but to do away with the tradition as inessential to the spiritual life (clearly stated in his work), and as a hindrance to the secular nature of public life (unstated, but is clearly implied).

There seems, in fact, no limit to the fantasies that can be spun once we agree that one can start over again, fresh, without the old prejudices, and from the beginning. It took a Ralph Waldo Emerson, however, to put a fine point on the matter and to furnish us with words that both endured (because they appealed to a certain romantic notion of human powers) and knew no reasonable and judicious boundaries. In his introduction to "Nature," Emerson laments that his age is "retrospective": "It builds the sepulchres of the fathers. It writes biographies, histories, and criticism. The foregoing generations beheld God and nature face to face; we, through their eyes. Why should not we also enjoy an original relation to the universe? Why should not we have a poetry and philosophy of insight and not of tradition, and a religion by revelation to us, and not the history of theirs?" The power in Emerson's rhetoric is itself primordial; it appeals to that same sense once recorded as "and you shall be as God." As if his hearers might truly start again in some new Eden, Emerson says, "The sun shines today also. There is more wool and flax in the fields. There are new lands, new men, new thoughts. Let us demand our own works and laws and worship."[23]

This refusal of the humble role of participating in nature, or participating as one who responds to the social life, or to the tradition of philosophy, began quite early. We might even say that it is a permanent temptation for human beings to imagine themselves independent of all that has gone before, or independent of the nature that surrounds them, and rather imagine their mastery of all that might otherwise limit them. Giordano Bruno, who lived in England from 1583 to 1585, likely had some influence on Francis Bacon. In a work he produced while in England, *Spaccio de la Bestia Trionfante* (*The Expulsion of the Triumphant Beast*), he wrote of the power of science in a way that now reminds us of Bacon. "The gods have given man intelligence and hands," he wrote, "and have made him in their image, endowing him with a capacity superior to other animals. This capacity consists not only in the power to work in accordance with nature and the usual course of things, but beyond that and outside her laws, to the end that by fashioning, or having the power to fashion, other natures, other courses, other orders by means of intelligence, with that freedom without which his resemblance to the deity would not exist, he might in the end make himself god of the earth."[24]

Bacon, in *The Masculine Birth of Time*, reflects on this mastery of nature as a kind of enslavement—a subject not foreign, as we have seen, from the commercial and political interests of his day. "My intention," he wrote, "is to impart to you, not the figments of my own brain, nor the shadows thrown by words, nor a mixture of religion and science . . . . No; I am come in very truth leading to you Nature with all her children to bind her to your service and make her your slave." This new dominion and enslavement of nature was to be accomplished by the inductive method. But it was not enough for Bacon to advocate a new emphasis of an old idea, which is what was done in fact in modern science; but, instead, he turned modern minds toward the notion that all this was brand new, that it effectively set them out on a course that had never been taken before, and that it required finding a way "of clearing sham philosophers out of our path." It is not the induction, or the recommendation of inductive method, that should strike us as significant in Bacon; it is rather his revolutionary zeal to wipe the slate clean and establish a master-slave relationship to nature. These earlier philosophers, that might have preserved, in some cases, a more balanced view of nature, "are more fabulous than poets. They debauch our minds. They substitute a false coinage for the true. . . . Will not someone recite the formula by which I may devote them all to oblivion? How shall truth be heard, if they maintain the din of their grovelling and inconsequent ratiocinations?"[25] As might be guessed, the authors of these "inconsequential ratiocinations" included not only Plato ("that deluded theologian") and Aristotle ("that worst of sophists"), but men such as Cornelius Celsus whom he tweaks as one who had the right idea ("devoted to a moderate form of research") but perhaps restrained in that he wanted to "introduce a certain moral control over the advance of science."[26] The restraint he had in mind was probably Celsus' opposition to the alleged use of Alexandrian criminals for human vivisection. Having made good use of the images of slavery and torture, we are given a vivid picture of what Bacon had in mind as the proper relationship between scientists and the world of nature.

Along with Bacon's multiple approaches to the dictum that "knowledge is power" are parallel sentiments expressed throughout the Enlightenment period, beginning with Descartes, and carried down to our own time.[27] Lawrence J. Peter said, "All science is concerned with the relationship of cause and effect. Each scientific discovery increases man's ability to predict the consequences of his actions and thus his ability to control future events." J. M. Clark, in an important study in the *Journal of Political Economics* referred to knowledge as an "instrument of production." H. G. Wells said that "Hitherto a man has been living in a slum, amidst quarrels, revenges, vanities, shames and taints, hot desires and urgent appetites. He has scarcely tasted sweet air yet, and the great freedom of the world that science has enlarged for him."

The Adulation and Distraction of Power

Science, therefore, was seen no longer as a means of understanding the world only, or of knowing it in order that it might be received with thanksgiving, or of knowing it in order to love the God who created it and to love his creation (Augustine). The motivation was not that of awe, and it was not aimed at participation; but it was gradually turned toward the desire for mastery—for power. As Marion Montgomery explained, Bacon argued that "the possession of facts leads to the possession of nature."[28] The former naïve sense of science was aimed, it might be kept in mind, toward some kind of relationship. For to give thanks, to love, to worship, to be smitten with awe, implies a relationship; and one enters into relationship in order to "participate," in order to "take part in" something. Notice that the very idea of "taking part" implies a limited role in things, one in which the "knower" (the scientist) enters into the midst of some greater reality. Power, on the other hand, implies a very central role. The "knower" in this case is the center from which the known objects take their place as so many spokes on the hub of a wheel. Control always diminishes relationship; it implies that the will of one alone is expressed, while participation implies a certain intercourse or dialectic, a "conversation" and a communion. The former diminishes community, and is inimical to community; the latter is an expression of community even when it might really mean the larger community of human beings along with all things living and inanimate.

Community, of course, always implies something that is living. But the power to coerce, the power to enforce one's will is always deadly. This "deadly" effect is a necessary thing, in that control is found everywhere necessary to the maintenance of enough order and organization so that life on earth is even possible. Because it is necessary, however, does not mean that it is other than what it clearly is: the restraint of freedom and thus of life itself. Every kind of community, from a marriage to a nation, can be destroyed by the heavy hand of control. When conversations only go one way, the other side of the conversation becomes unnecessary. When the Apostle Paul spoke of the "mystery" of marriage and the church in the Ephesian letter, he was speaking of a certain idea of a "body" made up of living members that became, in their union with one another, a new living body. All the members in this case "participate." Their joining together does not diminish but enlarges their life. Just as it is "not good for man to be alone" it is a very good thing for people to be joined in community. Yet that which joins them together is other than that which constitutes a law or a regulation of that relationship; and when the focus shifts too severely from the dynamic which joins them to the form that regulates them, the result is more death than life.

Nathaniel Hawthorne understood the implied relationship between power and deadliness. In "The Birth Mark" he was clearly reflecting on the growing power of science and of the growing understanding of science as a power. A brilliant scientist is married to a beautiful woman, whom he greatly admires for her beauty. Yet even while he admired her almost flawless beauty, he came to be obsessively offended by her one small flaw, a birthmark the shape of a man's hand, but of miniscule proportion, on her cheek. He determined to rid her of the flaw, and persuaded her to drink of a concoction that he knew would rid her of the tiny, hated, mark. She drank the brew. It rid her of the birthmark, as it also took her life.

Now the shift in science, in the case of Francis Bacon, is subtler but it is not essentially different than the shift in politics, seen in Jean Bodin. Both imply a new adulation of power or mastery, and the promotion of power as an end in itself. This shift, while easily detected in these early modern thinkers, did not truly begin with them. It began in certain theological issues that became for later times a sort of template for understanding the nature of power. Could God do anything on the basis of his *potentia absoluta*, or was he in fact limited by his attributes of goodness, love, patience, humility, and so on? Does his character, in other words, grow out of his power? Or is his power an expression of his character? Under the influence of nominalist thinkers, the chief of which was William of Ockham (c. 1280-c.1349), theologians were more and more persuaded that the dignity of God demanded that what he ordained he did so out of his freedom to act without any prior or contingent restraint. Thus "absolute power" took its place above the other attributes of God, all of which were subordinate expressions of his power. Though expressed with much subtlety, the pattern of thinking in the West tended to conform to the idea that the essence of God was his power. It was not long before it became difficult to separate, intellectually, the idea of worshipping God from the mere worship of power. Furthermore, to be made in the image of God came to mean, on some level, sharing in that power, *and in that kind of freedom, the freedom growing from the absolute power to choose.* The imitation of God was not then so clearly seen as participating in his goodness, his love, or his patience, but in his power.[29]

This had implications, as we have seen, in the realm of science and politics. But most of all it had implications for the very idea of community. It took someone as candid as Emerson to speak plainly on the matter (and I will have to say candid, though I am tempted to say naïve; but he is too brilliant to be naïve, which gives me the unsettling suspicion that he was counting upon the naïveté of his audience and disciples). "Let me admonish you," he said in his address delivered before seminarians at Harvard in 1838, "first of all, to go alone; to refuse the good models, even those which are sacred in the imagination of men, and dare to love God without mediator or veil. Friends enough you shall find who will hold up to your emulation Wesleys and Oberlins, Saints and Prophets. Thank God for these good men, but say, 'I also am a man.' Imitation cannot go above its model. The imitator dooms himself to hopeless mediocrity."[30]

This takes us back to where we began. Either society is a good thing or it is not; and so far we've seen nothing to contradict the biblical adage that "it is not good for man to be alone."[31] Yet the adulation of power always prompts the isolation and alienation of man. The contrast of Emerson's diatribe against imitation with frequent expressions of the Church Fathers is remarkable. They knew that imitation is at the heart of community. We learn language by imitation; every aspect of a culture is shaped and made habitual through imitation. And though imitation can be either good or bad, it is a power that forms community—both in terms of putting us into community and putting the community into us. It was frankly stated that the Church is built upon the lives of worthy exemplars, and the supreme exemplar is Christ who in turn lived in imitation of God: that is why bishops were thought to be necessary, not (as modern scholars often mistakenly argue) in order to protect privilege—at least not initially; and that is also why the word "martyr" has its double meaning—as one who dies for Christ and as one who gives witness for Christ. Imitation, and not isolation, builds humane communities. And it is through imitation that the idea of calling into community is mediated to the whole body. Ignatius, Bishop of Antioch at the end of the first century, expressed it beautifully in a letter to the Ephesian Christians. Concerning their bishop Onesimus, "a man of inexpressible love," "I pray that you will love him in accordance with the standard set by Jesus Christ and that *all of you will be like him.*"[32]

This is a power of a different kind—not coercive power, or the power to "lord it over others," but the power of attraction to, and affection for, what is beautiful, what is true, and what is just. These realities, are what excite the kind of imitation that leads to a true manifestation of a humane community. And it is the church of Jesus Christ that is established to give witness to the possibility of just such a vocation.

Life Together

THE IDEA OF EMPIRE is based upon a certain truth, and also upon a certain intellectual sleight-of-hand. This is true of all kinds of "empire," whether political, following the pattern of empires ever since the Assyrian empire of the eighth century BC, or the modern empires based upon bureaucratic organization or financial acquisition. The truth they are founded upon is that all communities entail a representation of the world in that their sense of presenting reality in forms of justice, equity, communal bonds, social purpose, and even beauty, is in principle unlimited. They represent "justice," for instance, within their community, not as the willful assertion of an emperor or a CEO, but as justice *per se*, justice that would be recognized as such by anyone concerned. Every community is, therefore, in principle an ecumenical attempt, and has an ecumenical purpose. Each community attempts faithfully to represent and thus to embrace the world. That is the truth embedded in every community, whether that community be the Roman Empire, the Ford Motor Company, the Mafia, or Warrensburg, Missouri.

The sleight-of-hand, however, consists in embracing this community—or, in reality, any number of communities—by the use of techniques that imitate the form of community but deny its substance. The substance of community is uncoerced association and a certain communing of persons based upon common interests, a common vision of life, common experience, kinship, and place. Communities arise alongside and within organization, or altogether without organization. Organization is even, sometimes, the occasion for community. *But community is not organization, and organization is not, in itself, community.* Organization, while both necessary and convenient, only imitates community. To the extent that organization grows to embrace more than a community can possibly embrace, to the extent that its ambition reaches to the level of empire, it only plagiarizes community and most of the time becomes inimical to true community. Community requires a certain scale, because the human experience is limited; but the reach of community, through the sympathetic bonds and the infectious vision of neighboring communities is, in principle, unlimited. Its openness to the world implies an ecumenical goal, while its limited scale implies that it is always rooted in real persons located in real places.[1]

The basis of such a community in the West, of course, was the Church. The Church grounded community in a comprehensive, unifying, and catholic reality; at the same time it is embodied in the local and particular. The ancient Nicene Creed defines the Church by its four "marks": it is the "One," "Holy," "Catholic," and "Apostolic" Church. In that it is Apostolic and Holy, it is particular; in that it is One and Catholic, it is open and universal. That it has "room" for different "ways" within its one Way is important; but what is different from the multiculturalism that has taken root in the West, especially, is that it is precisely the one Way, the one God, and the common understanding of humanity and the world, that makes room for the "many ways."

While in Taiwan a number of years ago, I became acquainted with a young man, a Baptist seminary student by the name of Job Sh'r. He was an intellectual, and had a deep interest in the cultural history

of his own Chinese people; and he was a convert to Christianity. It
bothered him that people would say that by becoming a Christian
he was adopting a Western way of thinking and living. "You don't
abandon a five-thousand year old culture," he said, "as if it is worth-
less." But that was not how he thought of his own decision to follow
One who was "the light that illuminates every man that comes into
the world." He knew that the early Western Christians had not abandoned their culture, and their wise men, but had seen them as aids
in further understanding the true meaning of their new faith. Justin
Martyr, Clement of Alexandria, Origen, and Augustine of Hippo, had
all learned from Heraclitus, Plato, the Neoplatonists, the Stoics, Aristotle, and others. Job knew all of this, and had considered it deeply
when thinking about his own conversion and whether he should see
his turn to Christ as an abandonment of his patrimony, his country,
and his rich, ancient, cultural heritage.

Once we were having a long conversation on this subject at night,
out on a hillside overlooking the city of Taipei. We could still see the
lights reflected off the huge red columns of the Grand Hotel down
below. Our discussion, as I recall it, touched upon how even a West-
erner could appreciate the beauty of the East, its architecture, and
its paintings, although I admitted that its music was a bit more of
a challenge to me. "Ah, but we have Western music!" he said, and
laughed as if to say that some of it was not all that much of a cultural treasure. I laughed in agreement. And then I thought about the
distinguished Oriental musicians that had so recently enjoyed great
success performing the music of Bach, Beethoven, and Mozart—the
European masters. The cultural trade routes go both ways; we learn
from and are enriched by each other.

Somewhere in that conversation, however, Job said, "I would like
to think about how some of *our* philosophers, such as Confucius and
Lao tse, can conspire with Christianity in redeeming the world." These
also have a place, he assured me, even as Plato and Aristotle have

played their part in helping the world to understand the truth that Christ revealed.

Later I thought of this conversation when the postmodernists, so-called, and the multiculturalists began to wage a war of resentment against the possibility of an ecumenical culture. It reminded me that our cultural "ways" are not always lost when a greater reality is envisioned. After all, the light of the sun does not blot out the features of an American or a Chinese landscape, but illuminates them.

The Shape of a Humane Culture

A humane culture, wherever it is found, is one that takes seriously its concrete particulars and its universals. It is not one that has successfully captured the essence of these things, for in taking them seriously, that society also refrains from speaking of them too freely and too assuredly, as if they were not transcendent—as if they did not recede from human minds into some kind of infinite mystery. It speaks of them, but not in the way it speaks and thinks of other things, that is, in the way it speaks of abstractions—classes and categories of things, the speech of the laboratory, the market, the legislative forum, the organization and the bureau. The practical management of life requires the discernment of what lies beyond the realm of human action and what does not. Life is informed by these matters, and the human soul is even formed by the recognition of the difference between that which can be received with thanksgiving and that which can be used and employed.

Modern thought, however, has typically rejected this fundamental discernment. It wishes to believe that all things are subject to the actions and ambitions of the human enterprise. In other words, it wishes to believe that all things fall within the province of *use* or *usefulness*. The whole notion of piety, or devotion of ourselves to that which can affect us, but which cannot properly be used by us, has become either quaint or totally unrecognized. To be pious has come to mean "ostentatiously religious," for anything that cannot be used is merely *useless*. If we are to be the "masters" of nature, then the very idea of being lodged within an existence that we can barely know or understand is impractical. As a result, no matter how much we speak of "the concrete," we treat particulars and principles *as if* they were perfectly knowable and could be identified with their categories, with an abstraction like class or race. That is because, on a daily basis, life is habitually viewed through the lens of abstraction.

But a healthy society respects the particular in people, things, and places. At the same time this society attempts to articulate—in its symbols, its myths, and its manners—a certain vision of the larger, cosmic order. Thus it seeks to embody that order, an order that tacitly directs its institutions and provides for its citizens a pattern for their lives. Individually, this pattern of moral behavior is called character, collectively it is called civilization. When communities become intensely productive of beauty and effectively restrained by a spirit of justice, when its members sense themselves governed by something called "truth," we say they have a "high culture."

Over the course of the rest of this book we will have occasion, and I hope a successful one, to explore that mystery which is yet an undeniable reality: communities do exist, and they spring into being even in the most unlikely times and places. Aleksandr Solzshenitsyn described the phenomenon in the context of the Gulag Archipelago. There in labor camps and prisons men and women found a space where they could finally speak the truth and form friendships with people who could be trusted. Often those who are poor and oppressed share in a community life denied to those who are wealthy and "free."

We should hope to understand this as more than simply a rational process. The moment we think it is rational we also think it is within human control; and if it is in human control then why should it not be serving *our* purposes, or the interests of those like us, rather than those of others. There is the rub. The "rational" community—the community that is organized and thought of as constructed—invites rebellion and the end of community.

Community therefore truly and strongly forms only under the influence of something understood to be greater than the individual, certainly; but, more than that, it forms by virtue of something even greater than the community. If it were a rational thing, it would not be that greater reality; it would only be answering to something well within the range of human powers. Community may be chosen or constructed in penultimate terms, but not in any ultimate sense. There might well be mediating realities—we share the land, kinship, language, faith—but these are never enough. We are "called" together. That is the sentiment that recurs whenever communities come into being and whenever they abide, prosper, and develop, as it were, a beautiful life together. The church is understood in that way. And it understands itself as the type of the true community.

The metaphor of "vocation," with the same linguistic root as "voice" or "vocal," implies that greater reality to which we respond, one of a personal nature, who summons us to a time, a place, an association, a circumstance, or to whatever characterizes a given community. The image is usually quite powerful; indeed, the very idea of it is that the individual is overpowered by it. That is why, in fact, he can be part of community, because his vagrant, private urges have been subordinated to the needs and aspirations of the whole—whether that greater "whole" be a family, a city, a nation, or a sympathetic alliance of communities spread over much of the globe.

The metaphor itself calls to mind the experience of "voice" or "voices." In a striking essay on the nature of Judaism, *Judaism Beyond Words*, Professor David Gelernter wrote of how Judaism could only be understood as layers of tradition into which one is submerged rather like a scuba diver: "But you swim not in water but in voices: the Lord's voice upon the waters of Psalm 29; the voice of the shofar, in which mankind addresses its most urgent messages to God; the still, small voice that the prophet Elijah hears on Mt. Horeb; the dark voice of Jewish history, the 'voice of your brother's blood' crying out from the earth; and the intertwined voices of unbridled joy, the voice of the bridegroom and the voice of the bride—the sound of God's presence in the universe."[2] He might have added the voices of Psalm 19, by which

> The heavens are telling the glory of God;
> and the firmament proclaims his handiwork:
> Day to day pours forth speech,
> And night to night declares knowledge.

Christian writers would continue this theme. Notably, the fourth evangelist identifies Jesus Christ with the *Logos*, the Word, a sentiment not unfamiliar in Greek philosophy. Paul does something similar in relating Christ to the Law. Since Christ is the *telos*, the goal, of the law, He is understood as Moses understood the law in Deuteronomy 30: 11-14, not as some *thing* that can be discovered by exploring space, or by dredging the deep, but this word of Christ (or of the law) "is near you, on your lips and in your heart."[3] This word that Paul speaks of, is it precisely a word that one can hear? It is very good that messengers speak of Christ, otherwise how would the nations hear of Him? But immediately after he suggests this need for messengers, Paul says, "But I ask, have they not heard? Indeed they have; for"—and then he takes us back to Psalm 19— "Their voice has gone out to all the earth,/And their words to the ends of the world."

Paul's readers would have known that these words come immediately after "There is no speech, nor are there words; their voice is not heard." They are words, and yet they are not; they communicate more than physical words can say; and they reach to the ends of the world. The spoken word is necessary; yet in a sense it is only a suggestion and an analogy of the reality.

What do words do? Precisely nothing. They are signs and witnesses. They appeal to the emotions, reason with the intellect, and evoke the will. But they do not act—they call forth actions, but do not substitute for them. God's creation is understood as a word spoken which calls forth a reality that is, in a sense, its own reality; it is not a projection of God himself, or a fashioning of some primeval substance, but the calling forth of that which stands over against God, as something other than God. The word comes as "Let there be light," and there comes a terrible over-againstness, a reality that never before was; not a continuation of something in a different form, but the very *existence* of something unlike anything else: and there *was* light.

This is how vocation as the ordering principal of community is different from "organization." Organization does not call forth the moral or ethical dimension of society, it embodies it. Organization is a chosen course of action—a method, a technique, and a goal—that has been hard-wired into the system. It thinks for the intellect, moves for the emotions, and decides for the will. Vocation appeals but does not intrude; it points the way but does not compel; its power consists in that it *attracts*, not that it drives. It is attractive rather than coercive. It moves us as does a beautiful poem or painting, not as a threat or an obligation can move us. It is love, not law. In philosophical language, it has to do with the final cause of things, not with the efficient cause.

The Great Distraction

If this attention to a calling is the normal work of a civilization, and of any collective effort that hopes to survive for any length of time, then it should not be an extraordinary conclusion that Western civilization has come to a kind of impasse. It is a commonplace that what was once productive of so many humane institutions, even though never free from the scourge of war and the many inventions of human ambition, has in more recent centuries become productive of vast wealth and multiple wars, while losing the sentiments and habits that once made for community. The rise in appreciation for the dignity of the individual became an excessive "individualism." The institutions that provided widespread order became the powerful bureaucracies of modern states, and simultaneously the engines of conquest through standing armies. Natural law that arose from and was strengthened by a natural theology gave rise to human rights that were eventually seen as secular. These secularized rights freed the individual of obligations to any natural association—the family, religion, friendships—only to hand him over to the will of his benefactor, the modern State. The state in turn was allied to the commercial interests that thrived on the urban dissolution of natural groups which had formerly cramped the markets with their moral vision of the well ordered life and their notions of the humane use of wealth.

The effect of all this was to establish the idea that natural groups, or religious groups, should have no hold upon the individual beyond his voluntary participation. Thus it is presumed that individuals create groups out of their freedom to choose. Society is no more or less than the kaleidoscopic patterns of individuals freely associating with one another, joining and identifying with groups and parties that they privately and independently elect. A corresponding preoccupation, in modern drama, fiction, and art, is the flight of the individual from those associations into which he is born. For modernity, the new version of original sin is that we are born into a human family. Salvation consists in the struggle to escape it. We'll call this understanding of society the "Enlightenment" model: the belief that the proper ordering of things depends upon a certain "awakening" from the spell of millennia of tradition and common sense.

There is, of course, another view of society. It is one in which the shape and nature of social groups is determined not alone by the self-election of individuals, but by many complex, sometimes mysterious, and sometimes obvious circumstances that bring the individual into some kind of necessary association with society, or with groups within society. This is a more traditional view, but it is also one less reliant upon the obvious fiction that the private person either comes into this world, or remains for long in this world, without social circumstances that are determined well before the person arrives on the scene. One is born to a family, lives in a particular place, speaks a certain language, is subject to a particular legal and cultural tradition, is judged by standards of conduct, manners, and morals, not at all of one's own making or choosing. One is even identified physically with a particular human genetic pool, based upon appearance alone, to be forever identified with that group at some level. All of these kinds of selection take place altogether apart from, and long before, the human person who in reality is left with a narrow (but nonetheless significant) range of choices to make in life. We'll call this the "Natural" understanding of society, since it embodies elements of common reason that assume nature is not out to fool us, but provides clues to the real meaning of things.

In this latter, Natural model, common sense and humility play a large part. In the former Enlightenment model, the aspirations of the human spirit and the longing for distinction play the major role. In the Enlightenment model, there is the temptation to minimize the obvious hold that larger circumstances have upon the private person. In Natural view, however, there emerges a certain intuition that the private will of the individual does not work alone in a world of infinite possibilities, but the person works within a larger context into which he or she is drawn or sent.

In this latter view, the life-forming question is not "What shall I make of myself?" or "What do I want out of life?" It is more nearly, "How shall I enter wisely and profitably into the life in which I find myself?" It is natural, of course, that this view of life should take on a religious character. In fact, it is almost unavoidable, given the quest for meaning in a world that extends beyond memory and foresight, in which we are incapable of exhausting either our own depths or world's heights. When it is expressed in religious, or even theological ways, it is expressed in terms of "vocation." No other term so well captures the sense that we are bidden into a world that we did not make and cannot therefore fully comprehend. It resists the delusion that we are "masters and possessors" of even the infinitesimally small portion of the universe that we happen to inhabit.

In the Natural view, the main task of human life together is to cultivate those habits and practices that allow us to "connect" with a purpose already inherent in the world. In the Enlightenment model—except to the extent that it has accommodated itself to traditional religion—the point is to liberate individuals and voluntary associations for the pursuit of "happiness" defined largely in market terms of private comfort, safety, and material or physical satisfaction. The Natural view is not surprised by the discovery of adventures and dangers in the course of life, while the Enlightenment model finds such matters inimical to its primary goal. Immanuel Kant speaks of the "courage" to think for oneself, by which he means the courage to rebel and thus "opt out" of the Grand Narrative of a given culture. Hobbes and Locke, two other primary Enlightenment thinkers, were less inclined to disguise their philosophy in the language of virtue. They straightforwardly suggested that the goal of public life is to secure such things as safety and the "indolency of the body."

Nevertheless, the Enlightenment model has steeped itself in the rhetoric of moral virtues such as "courage" and "tolerance," and the human ideals of "freedom," "reason," and "progress." That courage means abandoning the ranks of a culture engaged in the perennial war of resistance against barbarism, that tolerance means quenching the sort of discussion necessary to discovering what is the public good, that reason is reduced to a shadow of its former self, and that progress fails to identify its destination, does not detract from the effective use of words that still resonate with their older meaning.

What is needed in sorting out the distinction between these two models is indeed an Enlightenment, or to use the German term, *Aufklarung*—a clearing up, as of a clearing of the mind. It would be, in a sense, the experience of the Prodigal Son in the beautiful Lucan parable, who had liberated himself from his Father, severing the "tender bonds" in order to realize himself in a Far Country. There he finds himself feeding with the swine and suddenly he—as the scripture says so frugally and beautifully—"comes to himself." This is the *Aufklarung* we need. Perhaps the present crisis provides that moment of clarity in which we can once again hear a voice and rediscover the meaning of "vocation" as a call to our true home.

Up to this point, I have attempted to call attention to habits of mind that are so much with us that we are hardly aware of how powerfully they shape our lives. If life as we know it is fundamentally thought to be an organized existence, that is, one that has been chosen (at least by some) and coerced (upon many others), then there is much room for either regret that we did not choose otherwise or resentment that life is so "poorly organized." The apparent answer to forces that afflict us is, of course, the use of countervailing force of some kind. Thus the predisposition of life, understood in this way, will favor the use of force, and the result is often violence. Or one might say more accurately that the whole of this predisposition is one that aims toward violence in the long run.

This is not a rosy view of modern times or of the modern predisposition. It does not remind us readily of the triumphalism and bold optimism of Kant or Locke at the dawn of what was then so confidently called "Enlightenment." In fact the very use of the term "enlightenment" was intended as a kind of propaganda, advertising humanity's release from the bondage of the church and its superstitions in what was supposed to be a dark and narrow former age. But propaganda eventually catches up with its sponsors, and the truth of the modern enlightenment presuppositions was bound to be sorely tested in a century (the twentieth) that opened upon the slaughter of Europe's youth after what seems now like a comedy of errors, but which should perhaps be termed a "tragedy of errors." Times continued in that vein of savagery, still advertising its faith in "progress" but mainly showing a penchant for progress in the invention of weapons of mass slaughter. Of course, one might justifiably counter that late modernity has also brought extraordinary progress in medicine, even if its professed march toward peace and justice turned out to be a hollow promise. However, I must agree with the theologian Jürgen Moltmann that to observe the progress of modern technology and economics without also observing the sub-modernity of the oppressed and suffering is to see an incomplete picture and basically to hide the truth of our times.

Modernity and submodernity

In two books, *The Coming of God* and *God for a Secular Society*, the famous German theologian Jürgen Moltmann has dealt with the subject of modernity in terms of its neglected "other side." What modern people think of themselves and their times is one thing; but the unintended consequences of their actions and their mode of living is quite something else. The modern world is one in which the leaders, the opinion-makers, and people generally of the more affluent nations consider that they are succeeding in "organizing" life and achieving mastery over nature as well as human destiny. Its ultimate meaning, even if unexpressed, is one of the "organized human being who functions as he or she should, without resistance." It is the nightmare envisioned by George Orwell and others—a world in which the modern trajectory has robbed humanity of its freedom even while promising freedom. "Liberty and autonomy are what the Enlightenment promised in the sunrise of its era." However, in "the twilight of that same era, what emerges is the total rule of 'instrumental reason,' the loss of liberty and the dissolution of human subjectivity."[4]

The Enlightenment vision of living according to instrumental reason, even with its anti-clerical and anti-religious rhetoric never far beneath the surface, was nonetheless an apocalyptic vision. It sought a rationalized, and therefore predictable, world: one in which dangers of human caprice and the unreliable consequences of human freedom are averted. In addition, it wished to "master" nature at large. This is a secularized version of the end of history, but nevertheless it spells the end of human beings acting in freedom before an unknown and unknowable future.

The consequences of these ambitions among modern people have been, on the one side, the elevation and expansion of knowledge (science) and of technology. While nature has been little altered, the advances in technology and science have been just spectacular enough to have become a convincing "down-payment" on the exaggerated promise of mastering nature. Far from being an accomplished fact, the mastery of nature has at least become a rhetorically convincing device, based upon remarkable achievements. Likewise, commerce has expanded exponentially since the sixteenth century. Political organization into nation-states, especially in Europe and North America have proved efficient in regulating internal affairs and fending off outside rivals as well as in laying claim to vast territories beyond their original borders. The interrelationship of these—science, commerce, and politics—has proved to be irresistible to the European mind. It has seemed that the world itself was obviously progressing toward ever greater levels of mastery through what Marx and Engels called "the administration of things" and toward what Comte thought of as the era of "positive science."

There was all along, however, an "underside" to this sunny estimation of human progress. The wealth of first Spain and then England and New England owed much to the massive commercial opportunities afforded by the newly revived slave trade. Due to the influence of the Church primarily, the slave trade had been practically non-existent since early in the thirteenth century. With modern times it came back. This time the world was overnight awash in slave-trafficking. It is likely that in the seventeenth century 2,750,000 Africans were sold into slavery in the New World—not the result of dark medieval ignorance (truly an invention of modern propogandists) but the genuine fruit of modern developments that called for the mastery and organization of the world. North America's own sense of an apocalyptic mission drove them to possess new lands by dispossessing old populations and bringing them close to annihilation. The moment the Civil War had accomplished the centralizing of political power in Washington, the agenda turned toward the conquest of Western territories and fulfilling the Manifest Destiny of an empire. By the end of the century American arms were subjugating far-away Phillipine islands at the cost of killing 600,000 Filipinos. Thus progress looked very different to the black slave, to the American Indian, and to the Filipino than it might to those who occupied the new nineteenth-century suburbs and road the trains that spanned the North American continent, or to the British and American shipping magnates or industrial barrons who were on the "receiving end" of "progress."

In an essay entitled "Covenant or Leviathan?" Moltmann spells out the meaning of this always-present option between the community based on covenant and the "organized" and rationalized society of modern times.[5] A society organized from the "top down" was not the only option, as Johannes Althusius had made clear in the early seventeenth century. Communities are made up of many over-lapping "associations," each of which imposes a certain order through its own hierarchy, its own articulation of the common good, and its own expression of morals and manners. These have much of what Bonhoeffer called, as we noted earlier, the "natural" as opposed to the "organized" or rationalized. These associations are held together in a manner that is described as a covenant, since there are mutual obligations among the members of society at every level in a "body" of people that is nourished by a common sense of what is good and just, as well as a common expression of what is beautiful. But in the rationalized society of modern times the emphasis is placed upon "power." It also emphasizes "numbers," and "standards," and "outcomes" that assure some means of "accountability"—that is, a subservience to the instruments of control. This emphasis is found in the natural sciences as well as in politics, for the sine qua non of "organization" in the modern sense is a command structure that yields the results demanded by the ruling "mind" of the human being.

One may well object that this idea of a rationalized and highly organized society is hardly the way things have developed in recent decades. Ever since the 1960s, the most remarkable changes in society have been the freedom of individuals to flaunt the rules of institutions, to rebel against elders and authority figures. Schools and home life are not "highly organized" but just the opposite in many cases—and the chaos in these local institutions have been just remarkable enough to convince many that it is not "organization" that threatens us, but "disorganization" and the breakdown of social order. But this is only true at the individual level and at the level of so-called "mediating institutions." In truth, individuals, even children in a family, feel liberated from the restraints of family and local institutions, and they are all the more subject to manipulation by markets and government agencies who often find the authority of families, for instance, to be highly inconvenient in the pursuit of a given agenda.

To use a common example, but one that I think makes the point, it was once considered taboo to advertise directly to children. Business felt the need to respect the "shield" of parental authority in the use of family money. In the United States, at least, the point need not be documented since everyone knows that today children are more often than not the prime target of television commercials and, in recent years, businesses that profit from the sale of goods to children follow them right into the school building and the classroom. Therefore, while even businesses and government agencies may eventually fail from the general fragmentation of society, in the shorter run they benefit from the expanded ability to trespass on social territory once reserved for families and other local institutions. So the dissolving of institutions once considered essential to social order (and by most people they are still likely seen in that light) often proves to aid in larger designs to "organize" commercial and governmental enterprises. And the larger aim, then, is still that of undergirding and strengthening the organized, over against the natural.

In the next four chapters, I would like for us to explore what it means to reverse this antipathy toward vocation. Or—may I now call it by its proper name—the antipathy toward the idea of God, disguised often as a free person's natural antipathy toward authority. The term "vocation" stands for all of those experiences and insights that our lives are guided by Another, that we are responding not to inert nature that bends to our will, but to another Will, with whom we might live in covenant relationship, and to Whom we will be ultimately accountable.

I would like to do this by attending first to matters of immediate concern to the person who finds himself cast into the world and must begin to discover how to live, how to participate in this great arena of life. For this we go back to the idea of "attention" that Simone Weil has already underlined in her writings and of which some mention has been made.

Second, we will look at the practice of being open to existence, to the experience of others, including the experience of those who have the perspective of other generations. This is properly called toleration; but it is not the same as the toleration that has been promoted as adjunct to the growth of nation-states in modern times, that serves the further fragmentation of public life, and that brings any important theological or moral conversation to an end. Instead, we have in mind here the practices that come naturally out of the presuppositions of the Judeo-Christian sense of the world and the human intellectual task.

Third, we will examine the pole of inquiry that delivers us from synthetic abstractions and causes us to delve into the mystery of the particular. This we will do by examining the idea of "place" in human thought, human work, and human action. Vocation is addressed to people who are found in a particular place, and no matter where or how they are called, the vocation necessarily relates to the situation, the people, and the circumstance in which they are found. We are not only called *to* something, we are called *from* something and from some place. Modernity has displayed a peculiar antipathy toward the idea of place; the release from the excesses and the diseases of modernity require that we understand why that has been the case, and why we must achieve a new appreciation for "place."

Finally, we will look at the precise opposite of the notion of "place" and the "particular." The idea of "rest" in religious and theological thought represents the goal, the *telos* of human life. It is an idea that seeks to *tie things together*, to provide a sense of the common goal of all things, and the reconciliation of all things in God.

By beginning with "attention," therefore, we see attention directed first toward others (which is the heart of toleration), then toward that from whence we come and in which we have by accident of birth or circumstances been rooted, and finally toward that which calls us to our destiny. Here is a literal picture of the community that is in any real sense men and women communing together about life: nourished and informed by virtue of their rootedness, oriented toward their destiny, and open in love toward one another—this is the succinct meaning of community, the aim of which is to provide space and give nourishment to the human spirit.

— 8 —

Attention

THE APPROPRIATE RESPONSE TO VOCATION, from the psychological point of view, can best be described as "attention." This is a matter that we have already introduced in connection with the French religious and sociological writer and thinker Simone Weil. To carry this thought somewhat further, and give it all the *attention* it deserves, I would like now to go back to this point. Let us first think about Simone Weil herself. What kind of person would sense this need so thoroughly, and express it so eloquently, in our time? How indeed did she think about this need to give our attention to persons and things, ultimately to God? How is it that she was able to take the most common religious insight, so common that it seems a mere pious remark to the effect that the world suffers from "prayerlessness," and cause us to see it in a new way, with all its inherent power and weight? We shall look first at her life, briefly, and then at her thought on "attending." Last we shall see how this mirrors a prominent biblical teaching.

An attentive life

No one in this life will ever fully understand Simone Weil. But in her brief life, she left such a strong intimation of the mystery and the power of the supernatural in life, that we are bound to look to her as some kind of marker of the truth about God and the world. Yet to say this is to reveal something that would have surprised anyone who knew her in the midst of her young professional life, in the midst of her esoteric Marxist leanings, in her evident sympathy for left-wing causes. These always had an effect on her, just as (as one biographer said) St. Paul was always affected by his rabbinical schooling. It was in her concern for the poor and downtrodden, expressed in a secular materialism by French compatriots, that she was drawn steadily and, some say, unwillingly toward a transformed compassion for the poor that was no longer secular, but suffused with the light of the gospel.

Born in Paris on February 3, 1909, Simone Weil was the daughter of Dr. Bernard Weil, a successful physician, and his wife, Selma. With the outbreak of the war in 1914, Dr. Weil was mobilized into the French Army. Simone's mother, with her two children in tow, followed her physician-husband to his various assignments, making early education for the children an unsettled affair. Yet Simone, despite repeated episodes of suffering from intense headaches beginning at age twelve, excelled in her studies. In 1928, she entered the Ecole Normale and by 1930 she has completed her diploma-monograph, *Science and Perception in Descartes*. Passing her *agrégation* in July of the next year, she was made a teacher of philosophy at the girls' Lycée of Le Puy.

Yet for all her success and her steady rise in an academic career, she was an outsider. One might almost say that she was an outsider even to those groups to which she might have had natural and easy access. She was born to a non-practicing and non-believing Jewish family. In 1940 she protested the fact that she was excluded from a teaching position on account of her Jewishness, but rather than protest the injustice of that exclusion she argued about the "definition" of being a Jew. Since she neither kept the holy days and practices of Judaism, nor attended Synagogue, she insisted, she should not be considered a Jew in the sense of someone who did.[1] She seemed to court the idea of being an outsider in all regards. Though she is known for her sensitive and insightful essays on the gospel and on Christian life, she was never a member of the Church and refused to be baptized. This was the station in life to which she was called, as she saw it: "I should betray the truth, that is to say, the aspect of truth that I see, if I left the point, where I have been since my birth, at the intersection of Christianity and everything that is not Christianity."[2] Even more strongly, she wrote, "I feel that it is necessary to me, prescribed for me, to be alone, an outsider and alienated from every human context whatsoever."[3]

Her strong sense of justice, or rather her capacity for indignation because of injustice, was expressed early in her student days, and was shaped by her studies under the journalist and teacher of philosophy known as Alain, the pen name of Emile-Auguste Chartier. From her protests along with the unemployed in Le Puy in 1932 and her sympathy for Marxism and the trade union movement down to her wish to serve as a kind of World War I–style front-line nurse in 1942, Weil threw herself against the forces of evil and terror with such force that she seemed not to have the least regard for her own safety or health. On her moral idealism, Jacques Cabaud wrote that she was characterized by "a sort of moral need never to shelter herself from any struggle; a restless will to act, immediately, upon any idea that seemed to her to be good; a tendency to meet and to out-do violence and suffering by total sacrifice."[4]

It is perhaps her one-sidedness that both inspires and repels modern people, who look upon her with a sense of wonder bordering on joy, and at the same time a sense of shock. Her one-sidedness became apparent in her rejection of Judaism as a kind of ancient and violent religion of power and force, and at the same time of the institutional Church, with its organization and its sacraments. She expressed preference for the Cathars, the Gnostics, and even some sympathy for the Manichaeans, to say nothing of the admiration she frequently expressed for the Taoists, the Hindus, the Pythagoreans, and the Stoics. She seemed to focus upon the kind of transcendence which she believed came to an acute articulation in the Mediterranian civilizations and was at one point masterfully refined by Plato.

Her interest in specifically Christian themes comes after, or in some sense along with, these other spiritual probings. As early as 1935, her meditations on certain aspects of Christianity comes into view. By 1938, as George Panichas points out, "her writings show strong religious concerns, with an emphasis on the supernatural, though her interest in social and political problems and organization continues."[5] This intense turn toward religious expression in her writings seems to have been occasioned by a spirtual encounter in the spring, around Easter of that year. She went for a ten-day stay at the Benedictine Abbey of Solesmes, which is, as Panichas points out, "famous for its Gregorian plainchant." There she experienced a "mystical revelation." At about this same time, she was introduced to the seventeenth-century English metaphysical poets and read George Herbert's poem "Love." In her "Spiritual Autobiography," she revealed the pivotal role of this poem in her spiritual awakening. At Solesmes, Weil said, she suffered from "splitting headaches; each sound hurt me like a blow; by an extreme effort of concentration I was able to rise above this wretched flesh, to leave it to suffer by itself, heaped up in a corner, and to find a pure and perfect joy in the unimaginable beauty of the chanting and the words." This experience, she wrote, enabled her to understand something "by analogy" about "loving divine love in the midst of affliction." A young English Catholic there introduced her to the metaphysical poems:

In reading them later on, I discovered . . . what is unfortunately a very inadequate translation [the poem]. It is called "Love." I learned it by heart. Often, at the culminating point of a violent headache, I make myself say it over, concentrating all my attention upon it and clinging with all my soul to the tenderness it enshrines. I used to think I was merely reciting it as a beautiful poem, but without knowing it the recitation had the virtue of a prayer. It was during one of these recitations that, as I told you, Christ himself came down and took possession of me.[6]

In 1941 she met Father J.-M. Perrin, who helped her to explore further her growing convictions concerning the Christian faith. The next year, she was taken to a camp for refugees in Morocco, and then she and her parents were taken to New York. It was in New York that she began to attend Mass. She attended every day at the Church of Corpus Christi on 121st Street. Late that year, out of a desire to become involved in the French resistance, she left her parents and sailed from New York to England, where she took up residence in London.

It is important to see that all of this development in her religious thought took place in a rather short time, and not only in a short time, but a time filled with the war-induced anxieties of a refugee. During this brief time in London, she wrote *The Need for Roots*, which was not published until 1949. In April she was admitted to Middlesex Hospital. For reasons that are sometimes unclear, but have to do in part with her sympathy for the starving French people in the occupied areas, she refused to accept the increased nourishment that her body needed. In August she was admitted to the Grosvenor Sanatorium in Ashford, Kent, and died on the twenty-fourth of the month. In this brief time, between her realization of her religious vocation in 1938and her death in 1943, we have the collected and scattered writings for which this young contemplative woman has become so well known.

Christian discipleship

Perhaps because of my work in education, I have for many years been under the spell of a certain essay by Simone Weil entitled "Reflections on the Right Use of School Studies with a View to the Love of God."[7] She argues that the greatest value of "school studies" is that they develop the practice of attention and that attention always turns us toward God. No matter what the attention first turns toward, it is in its highest and purest form always a reaching toward God, or more to the point, a waiting for God. "The key to a Christian concept of studies is the realization that prayer consists in attention. It is the orientation of all the attention of which the soul is capable toward God." And even though these lessons in school "develop a lower kind of attention," they are valuable in holding the mind still and accustoming it to waiting until the light breaks and a new insight emerges.

I have been intrigued with how this essay offers an antidote to what I see as a prevailing mind-set among contemporary students. That mind-set involves certain prejudices about the task of study. Whether one receives something of value from the study of a subject depends upon whether it is instantly accessible to the mind. So the student who wants to convey the idea that he has a high "I.Q." claims hardly to study at all—things fall into the mind without study; it is an innate virtue. Or a student claims *not* to have an aptitude for something if it requires effort to understand. This is the obverse side of the same attitude—mental achievements are worthy in inverse proportion to the effort required. Or the student claims not to "like" a certain subject and thinks that sufficient reason to avoid it. I once encountered a graduate student who had an outstanding undergraduate record (I emphasize *record* because I know how tenuous the relationship is between the record and the performance), and said, after reading a few pages of the Angelic Doctor, "I don't like Thomas Aquinas." So much for seven centuries of Christian intellectual tradition; it evidently, in the minds of some, can be dismissed for no more substantial reason than the fact that it does not suit a student's taste.

But Simone Weil rejects the idea that one should choose to study according to "likes and dislikes," or even that for which you might have an aptitude. "If we have no aptitude or natural taste for geometry, this does not mean that our faculty for attention will not be developed by wrestling with a problem or studying a theorem." The point is to develop a habit and disposition of the mind; when one has to overcome a resistance within, either on account of taste or mental readiness, "it is almost an advantage."[8]

What if you don't succeed in solving the geometric problem, or understanding the poem? "Never in any case whatever is a genuine effort of the attention wasted." It has its effect in prayer—all attention lets in a "spiritual light." Even that has its downward working influence on the intelligence, "for all spiritual light lightens the mind."[9]

Students, therefore, she insists, must be sincere in their efforts. They must not be (to use the term we have been using in this context) *distracted*. They should work "without any wish to gain good marks," for instance. It is necessary to attend clearly to the true object of your study, not to have one eye upon an irrelevant and abstract recognition of one's study. One's attention should not be diluted by abstract representations of achievement, but rather intent on the achievement itself. One's attention should be held in place by the "line AB" not the grade "A" or "B." The former constitutes attention, the latter a distraction.

Further, we must pay attention with a thought of discovering our mistakes. The temptation is to avert our eyes from this, for it is painful to discover mistakes. But, "no knowledge is more to be desired." It is precisely in going back to the point of our error, both intellectually and morally, that we can set out more confidently and strongly on the right path, giving our energies to what is fruitful rather than subconsciously justifying what is unfruitful and wasteful, if not destructive. Direction counts for everything. No matter where you begin, you can be set out on a journey toward the truth that is the most important goal for any person. "The solution of a geometry problem does not in itself constitute a precious gift." But since it is a "little fragment of particular truth, it is a pure image of the unique, eternal, and living

Truth, the very Truth that once in a human voice declared: 'I am the Truth.'"[10]

In Simone Weil's writings—in this piece about school studies and in others I will mention as well—the word "attention" is not so much analyzed as it is applied. The question "What is attention?" does not come up directly, but the answer to it lies in dozens of examples and applications as well as moral encouragements. She even shapes the idea through mythical or fantastic illustration. For example, she tells of an "Eskimo story" of the origin of light: "In the eternal darkness, the crow, unable to find any food, longed for light, and the earth was illumined." Attention, for Weil, is in part seeing the correspondence between desire and reality. That is not to say, of course, it has to do with the most superficial desires but with the deep desires of the human heart. It is related to faith in that "the best support for faith is the guarantee that if we ask our Father for bread, he does not give us a stone."[11]

Attention, as Weil uses it, does not mean the conforming of reality to the desire or will. This indeed is the piece of modernity that so-called "postmodernism" attempts to save. Instead, attention means the overthrowing of "vain imaginations," the disposal of a self-centered view of existence. "To give up our imaginary position as the center [of the world], to renounce it, not only intellectually but in the imaginative part of the soul, that means to awaken to what is real and eternal, to see the true light and hear the true silence." The purpose and end of attention is a transformation in which reality awakens within us, pushing aside the unreal and selfish dreams which had kept us subdued in unwakefulness. "It is a transformation," she explains, "analogous to that which takes place in the dusk of evening on a road, where we suddenly discern as a tree what we had at first seen as a stooping man; or where we suddenly recognize as a rustling of leaves what we thought at first was whispering voices. We see the same colours; we hear the same sounds, but not in the same way."[12]

The centrality of "attention" in the teachings of Jesus

The idea of attention is central to the teachings of Jesus. It shows up most clearly perhaps in his eschatological teachings, which is to say, the central teachings of the gospel. In Matthew 24 and 25, for instance, where we find an extended treatment of the "time of the end" or of judgment, his concern is that, in the course of following Him, his disciples will not be dissuaded by the thought that the circumstances in which they find themselves will never end. It is the fear (of those who suffer for the good) and the hope (of those who profit through evil) that things will always remain the same, that there really is no meaning or "end" to the struggle.

Salvation, for the followers of Jesus, lies in enduring to the end.[13] And the spiritual initiative against "falling away" is always to "stay alert," to "Watch," or—to use Simone Weil's language—to "pay attention." The eschatological teachings in this passage from Matthew are followed by a series of seven parables that all support this same teaching. There is (1) the parable of the "fig tree" (Matt. 24:32), (2) the parable of the "days of Noah" (24:36-41), (3) the parable of the "thief" (24:42-44), (4) the parable of the wise servant (24:45-51), (5) the parable of the "foolish and wise virgins" (25: 1-13), (6) the parable of the "talents" (25: 14-30), and finally (7) the parable of the last judgment (25:31-46). Each of these prescribes an alertness and a watchfulness. In particular, it is an awareness that sees beyond the present to the time when "the master returns," "the bridegroom arrives," "the talent-holders will give an account." More than that, it is the kind of awareness that sees *even in the present* the coming of the Lord, for the natural question, "When was it that we saw you sick, or in prison and visited you?" has an answer in terms of the experience of the present: "Truly I tell you, just as you did it to one of the least of these who are members of my family, you did it to me."[14]

But the fact that this encouragement to be alert, to "attend" is the heart of Jesus eschatological teachings, only highlights a feature of the entire corpus of the gospel account, and extends into the epistles as among their most prominent features. Jesus encourages his disciples to "watch" or to "stay alert" in passages too numerous to list here. What this means is to keep in view the end in order not to succumb to the temptation to lose heart in the midst of things. It is the sort of thing needed in a crisis when the easiest choice may be desperately wrong, and the right choice may be desperately painful. To be alert, or "to watch" here means to hold in view the time of deliverance; it opposes the temptation to live with easy compromises, drowsily inattentive to the moral and spiritual peril of the passing world. It is a spiritual initiative against what we have been calling "distraction." Very often the "sign" that the Messiah has come is the recovery of sight to the blind. It announces the end to the inattentiveness that Isaiah described as the fundamental disorder of Israel, an inattentiveness occasioned by the unwillingness to listen or look.

Every really good teacher I have ever known has had the ability to convey to students a certain energy required for "seeing" things. That energy becomes a part of the learning experience. It consists of a loyalty—I might almost say a "love"—of something that is of such transcending value and importance that it is capable of making demands upon life, of changing life. Moreover, this relationship between teacher and the object of his thought, so charged with emotion, turns the classroom experience into an adventure, a seeking after something not yet seen, but knowing that once it is found our minds and hearts will no longer be the same.

In *The Heart of Philosophy*, Jacob Needleman makes such a point about Socrates. Why was he so important in the life of Western philosophy, Needleman asks? He left no writings; we know him mainly through the dialogues of Plato and the memoirs of Xenophon. But we also know that the *effect* of his personality, his teaching, and his life quest are immeasurable. What was the nature of that effect? What was his power to transform the lives and thinking of his world, and of worlds long after him. Needleman describes this effect as *eros*—the power of love. Socrates was able to "kindle *eros*, a longing for be-ing."[15] In Socrates was found a loving loyalty to something greater than himself, something outside himself, something of transcendent value. And this love of that which was greater than individual, isolated life—even greater than the life of the community—greater, in a word, than the world itself—this love awakened a hunger in the hearts of some who knew him.

"Attention," of the sort we are discussing here, and which is related to the biblical idea of "watchfulness" or "alertness," always has this quality about it. It centers not on the self, but on something greater and something outside. Its power is in its honesty, in its reflection of the truth outside the observer.

Attention and truthfulness

We can also say, therefore, that Jesus' admonition—Watch! Be on guard! Be alert!—means to be truthful. Jesus urges disciples to face the crisis, to make the difficult choice when there is an insight that it is the right choice. The inattentive, the one overcome with fatigue and drowsiness will choose the easy way, the way of drifting undisturbed into sleep . . . and into death.

It is moral stamina that Jesus calls for, made possible by constant watching. If one makes the right choice in a crisis, it must come from the habit of making those more difficult choices daily. "Watching" is, then, a habit of truthfulness. It is being truthful about the world and about oneself. It is being honest before God. It is a disposition against denial, and therefore against being taken by surprise when the truth and falsehood of things come suddenly upon you. Jesus will not take by surprise those who were watching for him. False wishes and deceit will only undermine those who insisted on believing lies.

Inattentiveness, on the other hand, does not come from an inability to see, but an unwillingness. We do not desire to see and therefore we are blind to what is true.

Isaiah was commissioned to say to the people that *this* is what leads to their ruin: "Be ever hearing, but never understanding; be ever seeing, but never perceiving. Make the heart of this people calloused; make their ears dull and close their eyes. Otherwise they might see with their eyes, hear with their ears, understand with their hearts, and turn and be healed" (Is. 6:9-10).

Here is the prelude to ruin—utter ruin—Isaiah was told. "How long?" he asks. Until the full effect of the blind eyes, inattentive ears, and dull hearts are known: "Until the cities lie ruined and without inhabitant, until the houses are left deserted, and the fields ruined and ravaged" (Is. 6:11).

The whole prophetic movement, that is, the true core of Israel's religion, was marked by a moral insight into the nature of God, carried forward by men who "saw." The more ancient term for prophets was "Ro'eh," "seer"—one who sees what others miss, one whose eyes are open. That describes who they are and it explains their power.

Once G. K. Chesterton drew attention to a peculiar feature of medieval Christian art, constrasting its depiction of the Christian saint with the depiction of Gautama in Buddhist art. While the reposing or seated Buddha rests with his eyes closed, the Christian saint's body may be "wasted to its crazy bones, but his eyes are frightfully alive."[16] Like Chesterton, I believe there is an important clue here. In the gospels we find Jesus opening the eyes of the blind. "Are you the one who was to come, or should we expect someone else?" John the Baptist asks. Jesus sends him word: "Go back and report to John . . . the blind receive sight" (Luke 7:22).

This matter of attention enters into ethics at the point that truthfulness (the object of attention) means to face the truth of pain and mortality. Watchfulness, attention, is the opposite of denial. Of course, one of the major ways we have of refusing to face our own pain, our own mortality, or the pain we might be causing others (or allowing others to endure by our neglect) is through denial. It is a device for avoiding pain. And among the distinctions that modern people have failed to make is the distinction between pain and evil. Evil becomes equated with pain, and thus denial and inattention are, without our realizing it, weapons in the war against what we have learned to think of as evil.

A certain school of medical thought, I understand, teaches that pain-relieving medicine actually retards the body's capacity for dealing with pain. If that is true, it certainly parallels the social effects of not facing painful truths. Society prefers the narcotic of refusing to face painful situations believing that, by refusing reality, it is affirming life. The post-Christian West has been, for half a century at least, bingeing on "life-affirming" philosophies. That includes the cults of "faith in our own positive attitudes"—the psychology of the Yankee trader. But it also goes back to the most deeply rooted of modern myths—one so deeply rooted we seldom recognize it as a myth—the belief in a general, inevitable *progress*, which is really a kind of belief in secular immortality. These narcotics have allowed us to march to the edge of a cultural and social abyss without so much as hesitating to consider the warnings of thinkers that are otherwise much admired.

Walker Percy once commented on the paradox of the twentieth century American's bent for life-affirming pronouncements—self-actualization, self-expression, the penchant for self-improvement and self-esteem. At the same time, he said, no other century has been more "death-dealing in its actions." Then he writes, "*It is the century of the love of death.*" He continues, "I am not just talking about Verdun or the Holocaust or Dresden or Hiroshima. I am talking about a subtler form of death, a death in life, of people who seem to be living lives which are good by all sociological standards and yet who somehow seem more dead than alive. Whenever you have a hundred thousand psychotherapists talking about being life-affirming and a million books about life-enrichment, you can be sure there is a lot of death around."[17]

The seriousness and the honesty of facing pain, on the other hand, has a bracing effect. It is the acknowledgement of a reality—an awakening and a strengthening—rather than the anesthetic of wishes. Intuitively, when we are faced with the honest picture of our situation—our limits, our mortality, and our pain—we begin to think we are on to something. Truth is the prerequisite of hope.

Think, then, how a sense of the world that we have been describing as "vocation" relates to this whole picture. If vocation is the opposite of a life simply chosen, from among differing alternatives, or among numberless innocuous choices, whether we call these "lifestyles," or "alternate realities," then it involves facing and accepting both the limits and the painfulness of that for which we are chosen. For the idea of vocation, you will recall, involves a pilgrimage in which ultimately we will be changed, and we are only changed by pain. Perhaps a better way of putting that is to say that to be changed, in any deep and significant way, is always painful. So the danger is not "pain" as we might assume in a therapeutic and anesthetic society, but the danger is distraction, that inattention that eventually leads not to the life-giving forces that come to the aid of the true pilgrim, but death—the death of a life that has first been made trivial.

The biblical writers—the prophets and the Apostles—knew that ultimately we become conformed to that to which we most faithfully "attend." And to say that we are made in the *imago Dei*, means that that is the image for which we are made to conform. Attentiveness, faithfully engaging the truth, is the beginning and the true mark of progress of a genuinely human life. It is also the process out of which a humane community comes into being. For the ends toward which we each are drawn, proves finally, to be the ends toward which we all are drawn in our several ways. Thus the openness of life toward the truth is also the openness of life toward one another.

9

Tolerance

A HUMANE COMMUNITY is an open community. It is not an open community in the sense that has become proverbial in modern times and among the fastidiously correct voices on the left. Nor is it open merely in the way political pragmatists of left and right would have it: that is, as a community that passes no judgment, exercises no discipline except as demanded by popular caprice, and achieves a perfect neutrality with regard to issues that have the highest importance in human life. Instead, it is a society that, in its openness to the experiences and thinking of others, takes seriously the strivings of all who wrestle with the foundational questions of what it means to be human and to live in community. For more than three hundred years now, the term "toleration" or "tolerance" has served the purpose of disguising the agenda of powerful states and centralized bureaucracies—those great engines that help to produce a mass society. And a mass society is one that is moving toward being indistinguishable in its manners, customs, and institutions, because they are all in the process of being ground to dust in the name of liberation, equality, and progress.

John Locke, Pierre Bayle, and others aimed to shelter the secular powers of the state from the corrupting influence of religion. Their method consisted primarily in assigning to religion the realm of private convictions, thus preserving for the state the management of public affairs. This arrangement took upon itself the cast of a new virtue. The appropriate response of the state to the competing demands of religious communities was "toleration." The state could be tolerant because it had ceded religion to the realm of private convictions, and later (especially under the influence of John Stuart Mill) the task of moral philosophy. This privatization of religion was seen not only as a safeguard for the state, but for the religious life as well. But what is not often recognized is that it was quickly being assumed that public life inevitably belonged to the state.

In conceding the private realm to religion, the state was giving up its authority over what it never really governed anyway. Religion, on the other hand, was conceding to the state that over which it had always claimed to have some ultimate authority, for it had always claimed insight into the nature of a just society.

Yet that is not all that we might need to know about tolerance. For in another day it played a different role, one that did not grind societies into dust, but built them up and caused them to articulate—through their various manners, customs and institutions—a certain truth about the life of human beings and how they might live fruitfully together in all sorts of ways.

The ideas of tolerance

"Tolerance" is two separate ideas joined by a single term. In the theological realm it best displays its natural duplicity: for toleration as an Enlightenment doctrine resists theology, and tolerance as a very old Christian practice helps to deepen and broaden Christian thought. By their effects alone, one can tell we are not talking about the same thing no matter how similar the vocabulary.

The one is a form of neutrality within religion and a form of bigotry toward religion. It wishes to neutralize the deepest forms of religious conviction, while pretending to befriend the idea of religion in general. I will call this the "Enlightenment doctrine" of toleration. The other is not a doctrine but a practice, one that precedes mature doctrine. It engenders an openness toward what is deeply held by religious believers of every kind—not so much the accidental forms of that religion, but its essence: the deep wisdom which (however incomplete) joins itself so convincingly to all that is essentially human and essentially wise, and thus permanently true.

So first I want to tell the story of the modern doctrine by which most of us have learned the ethic of toleration. Then, I would like to explore what it means for the Christian community to recover a lost, and often discredited, practice that nevertheless urges itself upon us for reasons that have much to do with the end of the Enlightenment experiment.

Many hold that toleration as we know it arose was propagated, and triumphed, largely as a result of religious wars that ravaged Europe in the early modern period. Wars bled Europe of as much as one-third of its population in certain regions. They also drove Europeans to search for greater stability, to adopt philosophies that offered certainty, and at the same time to embrace a general public doctrine that "religion could not, at any rate, be coerced, so one might as well be resigned to allowing such things to be worked out in the privacy of human hearts." Those were not exactly John Locke's words, but they represent his argument, an argument that was typically adopted in the English-speaking countries.

What is typically overlooked is that this idea of the origins of toleration—that it was a common-sense solution to the fear and discomfiture of Europeans as a result of theological disputes gone berserk—leaves much unmentioned. Early modern Europe was not only a place of tumult and stress. Some prominent thinkers have overemphasized this feature of Europe's experience in analyzing the philosophical shifts that gave a certain character to modernity.[1] It was also a place of emerging wealth, expanding opportunities in trade and manufacture, and a place that saw the immense consolidation of power in the new nation-states. Both the economic and the political opportunities benefited from larger social units. The more regions could be homogenized in terms of political loyalties, laws, customs, and beliefs, the more they became supine to those forces who harbored large ambitions that were to be fed by political subjects and popular markets.

Modern times are characterized by the growth of large scale possibilities. The scale which a political or commercial opportunist might hope for was mostly secured by the growth of a regional authority—the new nation-state—that gradually eclipsed the local, familial, ecclesiastic, and sometimes informal authorities that governed (and to some extent still govern) public life. The greatest obstacle to that homogenizing central authority was, of course, the authority of religion. And religion had, by the sixteenth century, so intertwined its affairs with the emerging political powers that it had lost much of its moral authority in the social make-up of Europe. After the massive loss of life in the Thirty Years War (1618-1648), and the English Civil War (1642-1648)—wars driven largely by religious commitments—it was not difficult to convince Europeans that religious authority was more a force for social unrest than it was one necessary to peace. That ecumenical bearer of culture, law, and learning, the Church, had now been rent from top to bottom. What once provided the framework of an ecumenical accord, could no longer perform the function.

Thinkers such as Thomas Hobbes insisted that the goal of social life was to provide peace, and a safe harbor from the life that is "solitary, poor, nasty, brutish, and short." No one could do that better, said Hobbes, than one to whom we entrust the sword of government: this was the true kingdom of God, since it is the only route to a kingdom of peace. Theologians could only complicate this arrangement, since they sought a kingdom that fulfilled none of the conditions needed by a world of constant conflict—a world that, in its natural state, could only be one of war of "each one against each one." Religion does not settle this matter, but the secular authority of the state does. Religion instead threatens the equilibrium of a well organized state.

It was apparent to many in the early modern period that this was not the only possible arrangement of public and private authorities. Johannes Althusius, for one, a Reformed thinker, had seen that society was naturally divided among a number of overlapping and largely informal authorities. These "associations" as he called them—the family, the Church, the collegium (those who work on common public tasks), the region—each impose certain disciplines upon the individual and demand a certain loyalty. These associations likewise mediate between the person and the vastness of the world outside; they make possible a course of action, and they interpose an authority in a way not possible for the individual. Each association has its own proper sphere of action and authority, its own status, and its own vocation or divine calling. The civil government is one. But it is only *one* of the authorities among a number of different and sometimes competing voices.

What was happening in the early modern period was the rise of a more comprehensive authority, which related, moreover, to the individual. Less and less did other associations interpose between the state and the individual, leaving the individual (or the family for that matter) defenseless against what Hobbes had frankly described as the Leviathan. One can see the effects of this in the growth of the state's ability to marshal more and more of a society's resources in waging wars against other governments. Moving from Louis xiv's decision to keep a standing army, not heretofore within a monarch's power, we can fast-forward to the twentieth century where giant states were able to populate enormous armies, wage wars continually through every season, and call upon civilian resources as if it were self-evident that no better use could be made of them.

Wars came to demand almost unlimited provision from the civilian sector of society. Why were such wars not waged in the past?

Technology is only part of the answer; the more important part is that the government simply did not have that kind of authority. Now nothing stood between the individual and the state. The individual was more than anything else, a citizen of the state. Other associations were being eclipsed by the overshadowing association established so remotely and so abstractly between the citizen and the state. With the results of the French Revolution in mind, Benjamin Constant said, "The interests and memories which spring from local customs contain a germ of resistance which is so distasteful to authority that it hastens to uproot it. Authority finds private individuals easier game; its enormous weight can flatten them out effortlessly as if they were so much sand."[2]

The modern doctrine of toleration played a role in all of this. The greatest and most indigestible of all authorities, besides the state was, and in many ways continues to be, religion. The authority of religion comes in part from its power to speak authoritatively about those questions that are central to human living: To what end do I live, act, think, and live with others? To what end does the community of men, women, and children exist? What is truly just? These questions are at the heart of religion. Men and women have been known, moreover, to sacrifice life and property to uphold and to give witness to a particular view of these things. The material world and the temporal life pale in importance when viewed alongside these most important of all human considerations. These transcendent values, drawing as they do upon the deepest and most powerful streams of human devotion, are capable of playing havoc with the orderly accumulation of wealth in a comfortable and safe life. The sixteenth century—beginning with its religious reform movement and ending in bloodshed on a vast scale—was evidence of this.

The early modern period faced two grand realities. One was this bloodshed, at the ragged end of a century steeped in religious seriousness. The other was opportunity in the form of increased trade, the exploitation of new colonies in America and new trade routes to the

Orient, the possibility (much of it presented by the emergency of war) to expand political power and thus expand economic opportunity.

Toleration, then, is the decision to set aside these very disruptive quests of the human spirit as a means of insuring order, on the theory that such matters can never be worked out in the public arena. But in the background of this decision is the rise of opportunities for power and material gain. The rhetoric was always against the bigotry of religion and the duplicity of the religious orders; but the secret wish, which was not to be denied, was to restrain such troublesome questions while wealth and power were so nearly within grasp.

If the religious quest is the central vocation for humanity—the call to hear what is our place in the universe and the meaning of our existence—then the lure of power and wealth in early modernity served as a highly potent distraction. The doctrine of toleration was the theoretical justification of that distraction. "The commonwealth seems to me to be a society of men," said John Locke, "constituted only for the procuring, preserving, and advancing their own civil interests." What are these civil interests? Are they life together for the sake of participating in what is true, just, and beautiful—for which something like a religious vision is needed? According to Locke, "Civil interest I call life, liberty, health, and the indolency of body; and the possession of outward things, such as money, lands, houses, furniture, and the like."[3] This he explains in his *Letter Concerning Toleration* in order to place religious interests stratigically within the jurisdiction of "the inward persuasion of the mind."[4]

The recovery of good habits

The modern doctrine has therefore obscured what might properly be called the *practice* of toleration. I decline to call it a doctrine because it is not so much the statement of something true as it is the preparation of the soul for that which is true. It has more akin to silence than to discourse. It is the habit of not cutting off your interlocutor before listening to what he or she has to say.

At the end of his writing *On the Perfection of the Spiritual Life*, Thomas Aquinas wrote, "If anyone wishes to write against this, I will welcome it. For true and false will in no better way be revealed and uncovered than in resistance to a contradiction, according to the saying: 'Iron is sharpened by iron.' (Prov. 27:17). And between us and them may God judge."[5] Such a sentiment reflects a habit of considerable weight in the history of the Church. One might say that some of the crowning achievements of Christian thought—for instance, Aquinas' *Summa Theologica*—would never have seen the light of day but for a strong sentiment of openness toward thinkers from other faiths and philosophies. It was in overcoming a predisposition in the Church against Aristotle—a pagan thinker, after all—that Aquinas made his contribution. He did so within the thirteenth-century community of thought that was famously populated by Muslim and Jewish, as well as Christian, thinkers. When he takes up the definition of "Truth," he proceeds by calling attention to various important insights into the meaning of truth from a number of sources, not all of them Christian. First he draws from Augustine, who wrote that "Truth is that whereby is made manifest that which is." Then he turns to Hilary, who wrote, "Truth makes being clear and evident." Then Anselm: "Truth is rightness perseptible by the mind alone." Next, without comment on his movement to figures of an alien faith, he quotes Avicenna, a Muslim teacher of the tenth and eleventh century: "The truth of each thing is a property of the being which has been given to it." And finally he goes to Aristotle, the pagan philosopher, who says that a statement is true "from the fact that a thing is, not from the fact that a thing is true."[6]

St. Thomas does all of this in a way that clearly marks it off from modern habits. He does not call attention to the fact that he is drawing from a plurality of sources that represent diverse faiths. Nor is there the lazy air of relativism here. Instead we find the resolute pressing forward to an idea of truth that can be common to everyone because it is *real* for everyone. It is inclusive not in the easy modern way, that makes its claim before any effort has been expended to find common ground, but in the more arduous way of the "Angelic Doctor" whose labors still constitute a wonder of human investigation and literary production. It promotes not a unity that is assumed and goes unquestioned at the beginning, but one that is found at some cost to those who search. As Simone Weil said, "Work is needed to express what is true: also to receive what is true. We can express and receive what is false, or at least what is superficial, without any work."[7]

This drive toward divine truth, found in St. Thomas, is not the same as the acquisition of truth. Josef Pieper pointed out what both the advocates and the detractors of Aquinas often forget, that his greatest work is an *unfinished* work. In spirit, and as it happens in form as well, it witnesses to the openness of theology always points to something deeper. It points to truth rather than holding it captive. This habit of thought has deep roots in the Christian tradition and helps to illuminate what is meant by the practice of toleration. It is an openness toward what is true, recognizing that the truth of God is true for all people, and to the extent that other cultures or religions have been illuminated by truth it is none other than the truth of the one God, the God to whom Jesus himself gives full and incarnate witness.

An example of this early practice is found in Justin Martyr (d. 165) who came to the Christian faith by way of Stoicism and Platonism. For him Christian faith is the "touchstone" of truth. He believed that the identification of Christ as *logos* in Scripture opened the way to understanding even pre-Christian philosophies as bearing a measure of truth. Explains the historian Henry Chadwick, "Christ is for Justin the principle of unity and the criterion by which we may judge the truth, scattered like divided seeds among the different schools of philosophy in so far as they have dealt with religion and morals."[8]

Clement of Alexandria provides another witness. Like Philo on behalf of Judaism more than a century before, he incorporated the best works of Hellenistic literature and philosophy in his own Christian teaching. The writings of Clement that remain to us contain more than seven hundred quotations from an excess of three hundred pagan sources. At the same time, it was perfectly clear that Scripture was his authority. His arguments would explore the world of Homer or Heraclitus, but then he would resolve the issue beginning with the words "it is written." Thus his thought was not syncretistic, but synthetic. There was, for him, a "chorus of truth" upon which the Christian might draw. This multiple source did not replace Scripture, but it illuminated its pages. All philosophy, if it was true philosophy, was of divine origin, even though what we receive through philosophy is broken and almost unintellegible.

All truth, Clement would argue, is God's truth. In his *Stromata* (*Miscellanies*) he wrote, "They may say that it is mere chance that the Greeks have expressed something of the true philosophy. But that chance is subject to divine providence. . . . Or in the next place it may be said that the Greeks possessed an idea of truth implanted by nature. But we know that the Creator of nature is one only. . . ."[9] While Clement's Alexandrian tradition had enormous influence on the church, the tendency toward a tolerant habit of thought was not found in Alexandria alone. Gregory of Nazianzus (330-389), whose ministry ranged from Athens to Constantinople, argued for the universality of the knowledge of God, who is "in the world of thought, what the sun is in the world of sense; presenting himself to our minds in proportion as we are cleansed; and loved in proportion as He is presented to our mind: and again, conceived in proportion as we love Him . . . pouring Himself out upon what is external to Him."[10]

An advantage that ancient and early medieval thinkers had in imagining the "openness" of Christian theology to alien thinkers is one that tends to elude modern people. The Aristotelian idea of *form* allowed for an understanding that was not confined to individual things. Form corresponded well to the Christian idea of divine *logos* and the Jewish idea of *Dabar* ("word") or of *law*. Such ideas were largely abandoned through developments in late medieval and early modern thought. As Louis Dupré has stated it, "Nominalist theology had thoroughly eroded the notion of *form* . . . . Christians had used this Greek notion for constructing their own synthesis of nature and grace."[11] This same notion was indispensable to ancient and medieval thinkers. Basil the Great (c.329-379), another of the Cappadocian Fathers, expressly uses this approach in arguing for the co-equality of the Spirit with the other persons of the Trinity: "Therefore, inasmuch as the Holy Spirit perfects rational beings, completing their excellence, He is analogous to Form. For he, who no longer 'lives after the flesh,' but being 'led by the Spirit of God,' becoming 'conformed to the image of the Son of God,' is described as spiritual."[12]

Modern times, partly a product of nominalist presuppositions that lost this connection between form and matter, also lost the earlier understanding of a higher connection among different ways of thinking and believing. Thus modern people tended to know no way of tolerating alien thought other than to say that all opinions are of equal value since they merely illuminate the mind of the individual doing the thinking. Or, to put it less starkly, they confined certain kinds of thought, religious and moral thought specifically, to the realm of the *private*. By contrast, Augustine could understand that his earlier Neoplatonist books taught him something about God, even though it was incomplete: "In the same books I also read of the Word, God, that his birth came not from human stock, not from nature's will or man's, but from God. But I did not read in them that the Word was made flesh and came to dwell among us."[13] And he continued to comfort Christians who are conscience stricken about intellectual "meat offered to idols," saying, "Let every good and true Christian understand that wherever truth may be found, it belongs to his Master."[14] Toleration, which in this sense, and not the modern sense, means listening rather than speaking too quickly, so that one might rightly evaluate what is said, was seen by St. Augustine as the normal habit of a Christian mind:

> And what else have many good and faithful men among our brethren done? Do we not see with what a quantity of gold and silver, and garments, Cyprian, that most persuasive teacher and most blessed martyr, was loaded when he came out of Egypt? How much Latantius brought with him! And Victorinus, and Optatus, and Hilary, not to speak of living men! How much Greeks out of number have borrowed! And prior to all these, that most faithful servant of God, Moses, had done the same thing; for of him it is written that he was learned in all the wisdom of the Egyptians (Acts vii. 22) .... For what was done at the time of the exodus was no doubt a type prefiguring what happens now.[15]

It is not true, of course, that first millennium Christianity was tolerant in any thoroughgoing manner. A famous example of a dissenting voice was Tertullian, who objected to all this philosophizing by asking trenchantly "*Quid Athenae Hierlsolymis?*"—What has Athens to do with Jerusalem? One finds skepticism regarding the role of other philosophies and beliefs in arriving at the truth throughout the history of the Church. But a tolerant habit of mind was, as any can see, an important part of the picture prior to late medieval Christianity when the talent for such thought began to be diminished. It is important for us to see that the diminishing of such a powerful tool as toleration came not with the "dark ages" as popular myth holds, but with the dawn of modernity. And if we should gain it once again, we must recognize the difference between an authentic practice and the poor substitute of a modern doctrine.

10

Place

*To tell you the truth, this is really my own fatherland,
and that of my brother, for we are descended from a very
ancient family of this district; here are our ancestral rites
and the origin of our race; here are many memorials of
our forefathers. What more need I say? Yonder you see
our homestead as it is now—rebuilt and extended by my
father's care; for, as he was an invalid, he spent most of his
life in study here. Nay, it was on this very spot, I would
have you know, that I was born, while my grandfather was
alive and when the homestead, according to the old custom,
was small, like that of Curius in the Sabine country. For
this reason a lingering attachment for the place abides
in my mind and heart, and causes me perhaps to feel a
greater pleasure in it; and indeed, as you remember, that
exceedingly wise man is said to have refused immortality
that he might see Ithaca once more.*

Cicero on Arpino, his birthplace

PILGRIMAGE is a companion image to the idea of vocation. We are called to follow, and thus to leave our normal habitation. But the significance of that move in response to a calling, and that journey toward something outside of our common life, is lost unless there is something to leave, a place from which we proceed. We are called, like Abraham, to leave one place and go to another—whether geographically or only in terms of experience. But the concreteness of vocation depends upon the fact that it is addressed to real people who reside in real places; and apart from real places, there are no real people. As the woman's lover said, when caught by her husband in the bedroom closet and asked what he was doing there, "Everybody has to be somewhere." Real people belong to real places, and places, like people, have a character. Vocation is directed not to some pure spirit, or an abstract personality, but to persons who are rooted in a particular setting, and who can be known in part by the setting in which they are found or came to maturity. Someone is able to undergo a pilgrimage only because he belongs enough to one place to leave it and thus produce some psychic difference in his own disposition; the pilgrim is moving *from* a place and *toward* another place. That is the difference between a pilgrim and a mere wanderer.

Many contemporary writers have recognized that a strong sense of place induces a certain seriousness and reality to the writing of fiction and poetry. Some have, in the past century, found this especially in certain Southern writers—William Faulkner, Flannery O'Conner, Eudora Welty, Andrew Lytle, Wendell Berry, among others. Of course, there are writers in other places who have had an almost equivalent impact upon an appreciation for a strong sense of "place" in literature. One thinks of the New Englander Irving Babbitt, the Irish poet W. B. Yeats, and the English novelist Evelyn Waugh, especially in his wonderful *Brideshead Revisited*. Going rather farther afield, one can find a sense of place in the novelists Chinua Achebe of Nigeria, Ian Cross of New Zealand, R. K. Narayan of India, as well as in the Russian novelists who faced the ideocracy of a placeless Communism and revived truly Russian literature, especially Boris Pasternak and Aleksandr Solzhenitsyn.

Since I grew up in the South, however, I am more acutely aware of what critics are saying when they claim for that part of the world a strong sense of place. When I was in the seventh grade, Mrs. Edna Cotton required us to learn Sidney Lanier's *The Song of the Chattahoochee*:

> Out of the hills of Habersham
> Down the valleys of Hall,
> I hurry amain to reach the plain,
> Run the rapids, and leap the falls.

That was the river and the valley I knew most in my childhood. I had seen the river as it coursed broad and murky through nearby Atlanta. I had fished in its clear waters in North Georgia. As a young man, I fished and camped with friends on one of its tributaries, known as Warwoman Creek. And I could hear the river sing because I had heard it sung from the time I was a child—and I knew the words of its song, passed down through generations.

I knew that once upon a time my forebears had a hand in reaching the shores of the Chattahoochee by rail. The rail was to be laid from Augusta to the Chattahoochee. About three-quarters of the way, in the 1840s, they hit a snag. Farmers near Covington refused to sell their land to the railroad company. That's where my great-great-great uncle, named William Denson Conyers, came in. He bought the land at what the farmers considered a fair price, and sold it to the railway, who showed their appreciation by naming the station "Conyers Station." Today it is Conyers. Where the line ended on the Chattahoochee River was known first as Terminus, then Marthasville, and finally Atlanta.

One more story will help me express what I hope to say about the importance of place in regard to the traditional, or "humane" and "vocational" community. It is another story that I was acquainted with through most of my life. In this case, the story illustrates the power of "place" in a rather negative way. One might say that in modern total war, there is the recognition that place has a certain power and the enemy must be overcome by eradicating his places.

On the eastern rim of the Chattahoochee basin is (one might almost say, "was") the town of Cassville, Georgia, in present day Bartow County. In the early 1860s Cassville was a prosperous town of fifty-some-odd residences, two colleges—a Male and a Female college—and, they say, a lively artistic community. In May of 1864, sometime between Chattanooga and Kennesaw, there was a brief skirmish there between the two armies—the Confederate Army of Tennessee under Joseph E. Johnston and the invading army under William Tecumseh Sherman. Later General Sherman sent back a contingent of Ohio cavalry to burn the two colleges and all but three of the fifty-something residences.

My great-grandmother—newly married—loaded her precious wedding gifts into a buck-board wagon, including a large "secretary" that now stands in our living room. She drove the mule-drawn wagon into the woods, near an ancient cemetary, and there unhitched the mule-team and drove them away. Then she piled brush over the wagon and its contents, crawled beneath the wagon, and remained in hiding for two or three days without food or water, there saving herself and the few provisions that survived the holocaust.

Forty years later, this same woman, no longer the young bride who hid in the woods from Sherman's soldiers, wrote of a visit to the now desolate place that had once been her home. The piece, entitled "A Walk Over Sacred Ground," was published in 1905:

> During a recent visit, the first in nearly ten years, of my sister from southern Georgia, we left the breakfast table one morning bare headed as in childhood, for a stroll about the yard and garden; but as the morning was cool and cloudy we extended our walk far beyond our first intentions.
>
> We left the grove and went up the way that was once a back street of our village, and at the end of it had a plain view of the

old college hill, up which we had so often climbed in company with the friends of long ago. And as we viewed its steep and now rugged pathway, and faces and names were recalled, an irresistible desire seized us to tramp once more in the footsteps of early friends and classmates departed. As we reached the brow and turned to look back at the little village at its decline, we were reminded of Goldsmith's deserted village, "once the fairest of the plain," but now only modest homesteads mark the place where once were many prosperous, lovely homes. Across from this hill stood another, dearer to us still. Then greater became the longing as we again stand upon the spot that was home to us when days were always sunny and skies bright.

As we neared the grove, before reaching the exact place where the dear old house stood, we marked many trees under which we had played, gathered chestnuts and upon whose gnarled roots we sat for an hour's quiet study when an extra lesson, or one of unusual length, or difficulty, had to be learned. We found where once rested the sills and hearthstones of our then cherished home; a garden had been made and vegetables in profusion were running riot o'er the sacred spot. I did not wonder at the luxurious vegetation, for twice had houses of good size been burned on the same spot and the fertilizing properties of the ashes lent to the perfection of nature. . . . Scarcely would we have been able to locate the walks about the place, but for the brick with which they were laid, the gate posts even having been charred and almost gone. . . .

The sweet-shrub hedge, from which our childish fingers plucked the fragrant brown blossoms and treasured for days to inhale their rich aroma, was entirely gone, but there "the orchard, the meadow, the deep tangled wild wood, and every loved spot that our infancy knew." An old peach tree at the edge of the yard where once we knelt in prayer for the restoration of an idolized brother was still standing, but with bent form, that reminded us forcibly of our first real sorrow.

As we looked and thought of the past, almost mute with sorrow, the falling rain arrested our musings and we noticed the gathering clouds and knew that we must seek shelter. A colored family now occupied the once large kitchen a few paces from the "big house." And under its roof we found refuge, but here again came memories thronging, both sad and gay. On the spacious old fireplace had been cooked my wedding supper and there within those walls my sister had stood at the hymneal altar. The first just before the war, when things to cook and servants to prepare them were both plentiful, and the last just after, when kitchens and barns were converted into homes for the returning refugees.

The shower was soon over and after a visit to the old well at the foot of the hill, then known as Cassville Heights, we drew again from its cool depths and quaffed once more, and we knew for the last time together, its limpid water. Then wended our way back, the trees still dripping, as if in sympathy with tears that were falling and with voices too tremulous with emotion for conversation. It was an almost silent walk to Spring Brook, the adjoining farm and home of Lila Land Chunn. (*The Cartersville News*, August 24, 1905).

Notice how she weaves the lines from Goldsmith's *Deserted Village* into the narrative. The place, the old homestead at Cassville, not only evoked memory, but because it was a real place—where memory, common bonds, community habits, sorrows and love come together, its evokes song. One cannot simply describe it: to do so is too abstract. One must evoke the feel of the place—even if through silence. One must come in touch with what Jim Kibler, after the manner of the ancient Greeks, calls the *genius loci*, the spirit of the place.

The embarrassment of place

Now I have promised to write about "place" as it relates to the idea of "vocation." But so far I have only told stories and remembered songs and witicisms about places. But I hope that you will see that I did so in order to make good on my promise in a more direct way.

The first thing we have to notice is the fact that it is difficult to be abstract about "place." The only abstraction that works is this: a place is not abstract. It is the opposite of abstraction. More than that, it is prior to any abstraction.[1] Our world, the world shaped by modernity, is one that attempted to reduce reality to time and space—both of which are abstractions that derive their meaning from place. Even time, which seems at first sight to be of a different category, is understood in reference to place. Without place there is no time, for there is no reality within which things happen. And time, being only a measure of things that happen, unhinged from place has no meaning at all. Even our references to time are thought in terms of place. Time renders itself in a before and an after—that which we face (before) and that which falls behind (after). Thus, without the concreteness of place there is no time.

Modern times are characterized by a spirit of conquest. The discovery of the New World was thought of as the "conquest" of the New World by a large segment of the emerging modern population. The advent of new kinds of financial ventures (joint stock companies, for instance, which began in the seventeenth century) allowed a kind of conquest from a distance—the reduction of economic interests to the abstractions of stock shares and entries on an accounting table. Science began to be thought of in terms of its ability to "conquer" and to "master" the environment, rather than its capacity for illuminating the vast world and its manifold mysteries. Rather than serving to underline our humble place in the world, it was instead the new source of pride. It was no longer the tool of a participant, but the weapon of a conqueror. These changes mark a primary shift in sentiment that characterizes modernity.

The idea of place is an embarrassment to the modern mentality. One can think in terms of the conquest of time and space—and in some important ways it can be said that such a conquest has taken place. But remember that time and space are abstractions that draw their reality from place. When we are pushed back to the primariness of place we find ourselves in a very different relationship. We only "conquer" place in the most ephemeral sense. In a more real sense we are always limited by place. Not only do we have an effect on place, but it has an effect on us. It is always itself, and subject more to its own laws than to ones we might impose. We can improve it, and cultivate it, and build it—but it is always and only itself. We work upon it, and with it: we are its stewards, but never in any real sense its conquerors. Europeans coming to North America did not make a new Europe. It made them Americans, and as unlike Europeans as any race on earth.

This is the reason "place" finds such resistance in the modern mind. Abstractions can often be thought of as subject to "mind." But "place" imposes a limit. Modernity is about the dream of always transcending limits. "Place" always ties us to earth, to the land, to the dust from which we came, and to the good creation that is not our own creation but is made by Another. "Place" humbles us, but it also causes us to think (as Gerhart Niemeyer used to say) about real possibilities instead of possible realities.

For Flannery O'Connor this was a problem that affected modern attitudes toward literature. She put it this way: "The Manicheans separated spirit and matter. To them all material things were evil. They sought pure spirit [which is the same as pure abstraction] and tried to approach the infinite directly without any mediation of matter. This is also pretty much the modern spirit, and for the sensibility infected with it, fiction is hard if not impossible to write because fiction is so very much an incarnational art."

Yet "place" is not the same as "nature" in the Romantic or the Transcendentalist traditions. The notion that what is primitive, what is natural, in the uncultivated sense, is somehow superior to that which has been subject to cultivation and refinement is, of course, a part of the modern resistance to restraints of any kind. It was, only in part, a reaction against Enlightenment rationalism. In a more strict sense, it was an expression of Enlightenment desire for human autonomy. Thus, the idea of "place" we speak of here is not the Romantic's ideal of a spot in the wilderness, or the primitive virtues of uncultivated humanity. Place, instead, as James Kibler showed in his *Our Father's Fields*,[2] is a piece of nature that has been perfected through the use and cultivation and dwelling of generations of families. It is very often a "built" place and a place of habitation, such as Versailles or the Vatican. It is almost always associated with community.

William Gilmore Simms made the proper distinction in both poetry and prose. He was often contrasting the primitive and rootless Indian, or the nomadic American frontiersman with those who settled a land, cultivated and "improved" its fields, planted trees to give shade to generations, built the dwelling places, and over time provided abundance for themselves and for a whole community. "A wandering people," he would say, "is a more or less barbaric people." They are rootless people; they are people without a place. Furthermore, this was a temptation to which Americans were especially subject. The temptation was to draw the richness from the soil with a single crop, and then move on to another parcel of land, leaving nothing but waste in the wake of such selfish endeavors. The point of cultivating land, he said, is to improve it—to leave it better, not more impoverished, than one found it.

One who cherishes place sees its natural setting differently than does the Romantic or the Transcendentalist. For Thoreau, for instance, nature provided a place to escape the community. It allowed him to be more "selective" in his company. (Reading between the lines in *Walden*, it is not hard to detect that he did not really like his neighbors; and even today—so they tell me—Concord does not really love him.) For the writer of Southern fiction, on the other hand, nature provides some of the character of the place, and that character bears fruit in a certain kind of community. For Thoreau, nature is a refuge from community. For the Southern writer, it is the setting for community. For Thoreau, the object is solitude; for the Southern writer, the object is life together.[3]

Furthermore, the community is not the "selective" community as Thoreau wished for, but it is a community of people as they exist, with all of their sins and shortcomings. Robert Lee Frost had it right in his "The Death of the Hired Man" when he said "Home is a place where, when you have to go there/They have to take you in." The power of Flannery O'Connor's fiction is that she did not clean up her characters before she put them on stage. And for her, "the best American fiction has always been regional" because real people live in actual places, with all their regional peculiarities. Thus Richard Wilbur defined place as "a fusion of human and natural order, and a peculiar window on the whole."[4]

This takes us to our final point. When Lila Land Chunn spoke of Cassville, she spoke of a place that she remembered, as did a few of her generation. Cassville is still there; but it is in many ways the deserted village that she alluded to, and there are no longer any alive who remember what it was like before that Ohio cavalry set the torch to its settled homes, its churches, its opera house, and its two colleges. Whatever one might say against General Sherman, one can say in his favor that he recognized the power and the significance of "place." And he was intent on leaving his enemies as few of those places as possible.

Yet when Mrs. Chunn speaks of Cassville, I think I am not mistaken to say that she speaks to us all: to all who have memorable places in their background, to all who can grieve, to all who feel the loss of that which can never be regained, to all who have a sense of that which can never in any real sense ever be lost. There is something about a particular place that is, as Flannery O'Connor would refer to it, on the order of the sacramental.

The Christian doctrine of the Incarnation speaks directly to this view of life. The ancient Gnostics, who despised the idea of the incarnation above all, were opposed by Christians such as the writer of First John who said, "Beloved do not believe every spirit, but test the spirits to see whether they are from God, because many false prophets have gone out into the world." And how does one recognize those false prophets? "By this you know the Spirit of God: every spirit that confesses that Jesus Christ has come in the flesh is from God" (1 John 4:1,2). The truth of the Incarnation is that the eternal and the particular are forever tied together. What God has joined together let not man put asunder.

The transgression of this truth runs in two directions. Let me state this with regard to the idea of "place." The first, and perhaps the most familiar to us, is the attempt to rise directly to the level of general truths and universal principles, and to assume that a "place" is an unwarranted limitation upon the freedom of pure principle. The other is to assume that virtue lies in the "place" itself, without any reference to that which is universal and catholic. This latter is the modern error of nominalism, which holds that only individual things truly exist. The "incarnational" truth of place is that particular places, with their own regional characteristics, and their own kind of community, nevertheless speak of that which is true for all people everywhere, and for all time.

"This knowledge," wrote O'Connor, by which she meant the peculiar knowledge of a certain community, "is what makes the Georgia writer different from the writer from Hollywood or New York. It is the knowledge that the novelist finds in his community. When he ceases to find it there, he will cease to write anything enduring. The writer operates at a peculiar crossroads where time and place and eternity somehow meet. His problem is to find that location."[5]

The mystery of place

Why does the Chattahoochee sing, as the Poet Sidney Lanier asked? First of all, because it is a particular place. It is a place you have fished.

You have waded out to waist high in the Habersham County branch of the river, and felt the smooth pebbles with the soles of your feet, digging at them with your toes. You did this on a particular spring morning so many years ago, along with friends who were better fisherman than you. It is a place you crossed every Sunday on your way to Grandmother's house, and generations of you have done the same. It is a place tied to a family memory, a memory not unlike those of others in your same community. You know words about this place; they are the same words that all your classmates and all your kinfolk know—the same words, and we think of them every time the place is mentioned.

But not only that. If we stopped there, at that point, we might be in danger of being pulled back into a kind of Romanticism that is just as modern and just as disparaging of the real meaning of "place" as the way Emerson and Whitman dealt with "nature."

A place is significant, and we speak and sing of it, because it offers to us a door by which we know what is true for all people, everywhere. It doesn't just speak of itself—though it never ceases to speak of itself—but it speaks of that which is truly catholic, truly universal—not bound by, but prior to, time and space.

The Puritan error was in attempting to short-circuit the particular and go directly to the general principle. Thus "love" attached to nothing in particular, and is mostly of interest in terms of its interior, personal manifestation. It becomes an abstract as well as an interior virtue. Justice likewise became an abstraction, so that in the name of humanity and justice, the Puritans and their heirs were often driven to do the most inhumane and unjust things.

The contrast is provided by those who thought they had an obligation to reality, those who truly believed in the incarnation. For them, the Chattachoochee sings its own song, but it is *also* a song about the true Object and Destiny of all things. Sidney Lanier knew both sides of the mystery of place, when he wrote:

The rushes cried *Abide, abide,*
The willful waterweeds held me thrall,
The laving laurel turned my tide,
The ferns and the fondling grass said *Stay,*
The dewberry dipped for to work delay,
And the little reeds sighed *Abide, abide,*
  Here in the hills of Habersham,
  Here in the valleys of Hall,

But the Chattahoochee replies:

Downward the voices of Duty call—
Downward, to toil and be mixed with the main;
The dry fields burn, and the mills are to turn,
And a myriad flowers mortally yearn,
And the lordly main beyond the plain
  Calls o'er the hills of Habersham,
  Calls through the valleys of Hall.

I have noticed that people often miss what Southern writers such as Eudora Welty say about place for the very reason that they miss this universal dimension. In explaining why she is "touched off by place," Welty said, "It seems plain that the art that speaks most clearly, explicitly, directly, and passionately from its place of origin will remain the longest understood." That much is widely recognized as a sentiment common to a number of regional writers. But she goes on to say something that is equally important: "It is through place that we put out roots, wherever birth, fate, chance, or our traveling selves set us down; *but what these roots reach toward is the deep and running vein, eternal and consistent and everywhere purely itself.*"[6]

Ultimately the mystery of place, about which Southern writers are so insistent, is no modern nominalism. It is not a conviction that only the particular is real. It is, instead, a reflection of the Mystery of the Incarnation. That is, God himself, made himself known, in a particular man, of a particular people, in a particular place. And he did so not in order to lead men to *that* place (as thousands of pilgrims thought), but in order to lead them to their own place—and through that place to the God who made them and *placed them there.*

11

Rest

IN AN IMMENSELY VALUABLE BOOK on the philosophy of Thomas Hobbes, *The Politics of Motion*, Thomas Spragens said that "the more one examines the logical structure of the seventeenth-century intellectual transformation, the more he is impressed by the absolute centrality to the whole process of a new view of motion."[1] He says this because philosophically the seventeenth century marks a change from viewing motion as the result of causes brought to bear upon a world that would otherwise be at rest, to a view of a world naturally in motion, unless some cause prevents or diverts that motion. Do we understand the nature of things from the point of view of things at rest, or things necessarily in motion? For Thomas Aquinas, motion causes us to reflect back to an "unmoved mover." But for Thomas Hobbes, at the beginning of modern times, the notion of "rest" is taken out of the picture entirely. The modern world is therefore understood as a "dynamic" world—always changing, and never to be understood in terms of objects at rest.

What drops out of the picture along with the beginning of motion, however, is also the "end" of motion—in other words the "goal" or the purpose of motion. From Aristotle to Aquinas and beyond, any motion is invested with purpose. This was often referred to as a "final cause," which means the cause "for the sake of which" something is done. Thus the world itself is suffused with purposefulness, with a goal, or an "end." And every person's life must be understood in terms of its purpose. Motion, or events, are then understood as fulfilling some perfection or completion. When we ask a friend, "Why did you do that?" it may be in surprised response to an act of generosity, or out of disappointment in their ill-considered act of foolishness, or treachery, or some out-of-character miss-step. We don't have to be medieval persons to think that actions have a purpose, or to project upon the world-at-large an expectation of purposeful action. Yet in our formal way of expressing modern prejudices, we see the world as full of dynamism that leads to nothing in particular, except accidentally or because the actions have been shaped and guided by the human mind.

Aristotle did not believe that motion came to an end, or had a beginning, any more than Hobbes did. What he did believe, however, was that motion was answerable to an end, and therefore to the notion of "rest" or "perfection" or completion. Otherwise, motion would be purely chaotic instead of what we typically see: namely, that motion gives rise to form and order. The difference for Hobbes shows how reduced the modern idea of the world had become. For the world or for human society to have meaning and purposefulness, it must be given that either by accident of nature or by the ingenuity of human organization. It is not often recognized that the so-called Enlightenment did not so much illuminate the world of humanity and nature as it focused very tightly upon those ways in which the world could now be managed through the increased powers available to modern Europeans. And those increased powers were seen specifically in science understood as technical power, through the vast expansion of commerce, and through the accompanying expansion of political centers of power in the new nation-states. These were so impressive to early modern thinkers (and to modern people in general) that they were tempted to see the vast world through lens tinted by human accomplishment. And at the same time they were tempted to lose respect for the vastness and mystery of even their own existence, as well as for the mystery of the cosmos around them, the mystery of the beginning of all things, and the contemplation of the end of things. It is no accident that modern people must disguise death, and make their funerary rites innocuous, for nothing so embarrasses the modern self-concept and the myth of instrumental reason.

The cultural meaning of "rest"

My own awakening to the importance of these matters in the lives of families and communities, however, did not come from the philosophy of Aristotle or the theology of Thomas Aquinas. And it did not come from the numbers of thinkers in this century, capable as they are, who are showing clearly the dangerous fissures in the modern edifice. Nor did it come even from those who, like Dietrich Bonhoeffer, have helped to point the way to a better life in community. My awakening came instead with the almost accidental acquaintance that I made with the writings of a literary figure from the nineteenth century. He was not one of the best known from that century to twentieth century people, even though he was among the best known in the 1840s and 1850s.

I became acquainted with William Gilmore Simms through the influence of friends. Otherwise, I would likely never have become acquainted with this forgotten genius of nineteenth-century letters. Most of all, I think, I would have missed his social criticism, which constitutes a kind of theology, for he understands society always in the light of its being called into being by God, the creator and redeemer. This social criticism shows up in explicit essays and addresses to the many university based "literary" or debating societies found in the South right up through the twentieth century.[2]

When I was, by a series of circumstances, introduced to Simms, I felt almost as if I had stumbled onto a continent that was yet unexplored, or at least one that had been abandoned and forgotten. Here was a first-rate literary and critical mind, whose production of novels, poetry, history, and criticism was nothing short of phenomenal; and yet because he had been a strong advocate of the Southern resistance during the war, was essentially exiled from public life and all but forgotten as a major nineteenth century literary figure. It was as if William Faulkner, the novelist, Robert Frost, the poet, and Richard Weaver, the social critic, were all forgotten and all their works sent into oblivion by those unsympathetic with their politics. Imagine what it would mean that the memory of these and their works were lost because they had been caught on the wrong side of a political struggle. Imagine the literary vacuum that would result. To me, it seemed that just such a thing had happened in the case of Simms. Therefore the discovery of him at this late date seemed all the more surprising. In fact, this discovery helped me to understand that the political upheavals taking place in America from 1860 to 1876 had the effect of erasing from public memory certain of the more intransigent elements that somehow refused to be absorbed into the post-Civil War American self-understanding.

He was, to my mind, as benighted as many southerners and not a few northerners were on the real relationship of slavery and race. Nevertheless, he resisted the evil he saw and often pointed the way to good, even if not always perfectly. Perhaps no more could be expected of the nineteenth century, or any century for that matter. Even the Great Emancipator, Lincoln, was bound by his provincial racism and less able than many southerners to understand the humanity of those he finally wished to free.

Yet because Simms was, for me at least, an unexplored country, I had only a few guides to help me understand his innermost motivations. It was apparent that he was deeply concerned about the American character, the influence of frontier life on the continuance of civilization, the tendency to allow economic interests to be reduced to money and commerce rather than expanded to include habits of generosity and hospitality and good husbandry. Like most Southerners, he was not drawn into debates about States' rights and slavery until quite far along in the crisis that led to the secession of the Southern States. That his interests were economic and moral was a reflection of the concerns of thoughtful Americans throughout the early nineteenth century.

It was apparent to me that there were some superb Simms scholars, already hard at work throughout the 1970s and 1980s on various aspects of his writings. Yet there were still only a few of them, compared to the legions of Faulkner and O'Connor scholars. Jack Guilds had taken a great interest in his novels, especially as they touched upon the westward movement in America, and produced the first biography of Simms in the twentieth century. James Kibler was the leading student of his poetry. David Aiken was responsible for much of the attention given to his most important novels, for giving attention to their place in the literary life of America and their continuing influence down to the present. In addition, Aiken was responsible, more than anyone else, for beginning to explore the religious dimension of Simms' works. He was the one who recruited me, as a student of theology, to contribute something of a theologians' perspective on the writings of Simms; and I have been engaged in this (rather as an amateur and interloper in the field) ever since, primarily by studying his poetry and his social criticism.

After a few years of this, and being drawn more and more to the rich theological and Christian wisdom that I was finding in Simms, I was given the assignment of coming up with a study of Simms' *Sabbath Lyrics*, a collection of poems that advertised itself as a "Christmas Gift of Love," and which looked to all the world like a seasonal publication with no particular importance except that it provided yet more evidence of Simms's talent and prodigious capacity for work. It was, upon first careful inspection, actually a puzzling collection of works, with many verses obviously related to the Christmas season, but with many that did not seem to fit the occasion at all. Several were about death, and specifically the death of his children.

It is therefore tempting to raise the mere biographical point that this consolation concerning the death in the family is the more general concern of the collection of poems. There must have been more compelling reasons to deal with this matter, I thought, than the mere recording of words of consolation for a Christmas publication. Of the fourteen children born to William Gilmore and Chevillette Simms, only five survived their father. From 1837 until the publication of *Sabbath Lyrics*, seven had been born—six daughters, and one son. In that same period, four of the daughters died: one was only a few days old, two were around one year old, and one was nearly three.

Yet the poetic imagination of Simms is engaged with more than the fact of loss and grief, as significant as this must have been for him. Rather he reflects upon the more general experience of life which these episodes of birth and death make both vivid and pathetic. He reflects upon the larger theme of the ravages of time, and he seeks after that within time that offers solace and safety from the general dissolution that accompanies the passage of things and events. He seeks for what is permanent, or at least, lasting. In this light, death does not merely represent itself, but it represents for the Christian thinker "the last enemy" (in the Apostle Paul's language) and that which most deeply marks time as unredeemed. The Greek god Chronos, from which we take the word chronological, is also called the destroyer. If time means only eventual destruction and loss, it can only gain purposefulness by that which escapes the ravages of time. As Boethius (c. 480-525) contemplates the ruin of his career and his cruel imprisonment, he writes the forlorn verses,

> One thing is fixed, by eternal law arranged;
> Nothing which comes to be remains.[3]

In the ancient and medieval mind, the contrary of this inexorable ruin to which all things run in time is the notion of "rest," which means that time runs toward a goal or purpose—an eschatological goal, a telos—that is secure against the ravages of Chronos. Thus St. Augustine could say, "We were made for Thee, O God, and our hearts are restless until we find rest in Thee."[4] Rest is not idleness, but, as Thomas Merton said, "the highest form of activity." Nor is it obliteration in death. That is why the Christian prayer, "Rest in peace," is not a concession to death but, in fact, an *invocation against death.*

In this poetry that includes many explicit references to destruction, loss, desolation, grief, and death, we also find the poetic grasp of that which promises hope, redemption, and rest. The birth of Jesus is then seen in greatest relief against the destruction of Jerusalem, the judgment of Moab, the desolation of exile, and the death of children. What I found in these poems, shaped admittedly more to the tastes of a nineteenth century ear than to mine, was the determined juxtaposing of the ravages of time with the contemplation of permanence. "For an Infant's Grave" for instance, is followed close by verses entitled "Christ the Conqueror." Next Simms shifts to the subject, not of permanent things, nor of destruction, but of how these two are actually mingled in life, how the promise and hope exist along with exile, distruction, and ruin. The theme seems to be that while life is effectively wounded by the powerful ravages of change, it is continually *shaped* by the promise of that which is its constant goal. The wounding and the healing take place simultaneously and in the same present world. The difference is between those who believe that the wounding is always mortal, and those who trust that the healing of persons and communities always will prevail in the end.

The social principle

Simms' preoccupation with permanence over against flux in these poems is seen in its strongest light when viewed alongside his social criticism of the same period. Two sources of Simms' thought from this period come to us in the form of orations. One, delivered in 1842 and published in 1843, was presented before the Eurosophic Society of the University of Alabama. It is entitled *The Social Principle: The True Source of National Permanence.* The other was delivered at Oglethorpe University and published in 1847 under the title *Self-Development.* These are remarkable orations, filled with revelations of his social philosophy and causing his poetry to become luminous at points that it might otherwise appear to be either obscure or commonplace.

In these writings, three themes can be seen as sub-themes of Simms' more abstract concern with the search for permanence in the midst of flux, and purpose in the midst of randomness. They are domesticity and civilization, the sirens of money and commerce, and the idea of vocation or purpose in life.

The reason the English prevailed over the French and the Spanish in settling the New World, Simms argues, is that the English intended, more than the other two, to live here. They built their homes and cottages, planted their trees, and invested in the generations to come. This is the domestic principle which is, according to Simms, the "true source of national permanence." "The progress of one man, thus endowing his little cottage with love and comfort, provokes the emulation of his neighbor, and thus hamlets rise, and great cities, even in a wilderness like this!"[5] The pleasures of home constitutes "the order which regulates without being seen,—the authority which is felt without being heard."[6]

Over against this development of settled and civil life, the fact of war, including the Revolutionary War, "threw us back in this respect." In addition, the motility and transitory habits of a people decrease their power to develop civilizing institutions. "In degree, all wanderers cease to be laborers. Their habits become desultory and unsettled. They obey impulses rather than laws, and toil in obedience to their humours rather than their necessities."[7] "A wandering people," he writes, "is more or less a barbarous one."[8]

In *The Social Principle*, Simms complains that Americans, southern as well as northern, have gotten into the fatal habit of reducing
social goals to money and social life to that of commerce. This has
a similar effect upon a people that motility and rootlessness have. It
works against the cultivation of institutions that sustain a life of refinement and order. A people whose life is reduced to commerce, no
less than a wondering people, is more or less a barbarian people. He
finds the example in the southern planter who devoted himself to "the
production of one commodity only which could find a market." Thus,
the "whole labor of the planter was expended,—not in the cultivation
of the soil,—for the proper cultivation of a soil improves it,—but in
extorting by violence from its bosom, seed and stalk, alike, of the
wealth which it contained. He slew the goose that he might grasp, at
one moment its whole golden treasure." [9]

The results follow. The farm family easily abandons the land for
other land that will yield crops more easily. And there is little to prevent this moving about and this rootlessness: "He laid out no gardens,
the graveled walks and tropical beauties of which would have fastened,
as with the spells of Armida, his reluctant footsteps—planted no favorite trees, whose mellowing shade, covering the graves of father,
mother or favorite child—would have seemed too sacred for deser-
tion—would have seemed like venerated relatives whom it would be
cruel to abandon in their declining years. These, are the substantial marks of a civilization, by which we distinguish an improving
people." [10]

Such preoccupation with commerce has its effects in the artistic
realm as well, which is the principle issue of *Self-Development* (1847).
The proper object of ambition is to follow in obedience to one's vocation, since "he cannot be a Christian, who fails in obedience to the
laws of his own nature—who suffers his faculties to sleep in sloth, and
stifles his peculiar endowment, which is his *one* talent, in the folds
of a napkin!" [11] Yet the interests of the market and the interests of a

person's "peculiar endowment" are often quite distinct, causing the
ambitious soul to be distracted from his intended vocation in order to
answer the less substantial voices of vulgar commerce and its "miser-
able catalogue of vanities." "And for such as these," Simms emphasizes,
"what years are sacrificed, what gifts squandered, what noble natures
wrecked forever!" Thus "money . . . through the most silly appetites,
becomes the master passion of mankind. It chains the virtues—bends
the moods—buys the affections—tames Ambition—subjugates Love,
and walks, the Universal Conqueror!"[12]

Again in *Sabbath Lyrics* we find these same emphases. "The Bread
of Life" is based on Matthew 4 and bears the epigraph "Man shall not
live by bread alone, but by every word that proceedeth out of the
mouth of God."

> Ah! Still in vain, the human care,
>   That ever craves the morrow's food,
> And seeks provision, far and near,
>   For mortal want and passing mood;
> That wastes the soil, that robs the mine
>   In sleepless march that nought supplies;

Institutional religion itself is apt to be swept along in the commercial trivialization of things. This is perhaps why Simms, while he
shows great devotion to the Christian tradition, tends to show little
respect for the church as an institution. His scenes of worship are
likely to be those of a shrine provided by nature or the home itself.
In "Forest Worship" he speaks of this tension between true religion
and its commercial immitation:

> Ah! Vain is that worship, whose vision
>   Still craves for the gold on the shrine . . . .[13]

The restlessness of modernity

The overarching concern that we find in Simms' writings of this period—which in fact has a significant bearing upon his later experience and thought during the war and afterward, when he had lost everything in the general destruction of South Carolina—might be stated briefly. The life of a community, if it is to afford those forms of experience for which the human being is made, must with some degree of success discover and cultivate permanence in the midst of the inevitable flux, restlessness, and change of human existence.

In his religious poetry especially, Simms does not underestimate the serious difficulty of this prerequisite to all civilizing habits and institutions. Death itself is the ultimate affront to the hopeful striving after permanence. Death mocks the efforts and the active life of community, tempting the faint-hearted to believe that nothing in fact except death is permanent.

> The soul, too, has its night, a perilous hour,—
> The mind its madness, and the heart its pain; [14]

Thus, in "Despondency and Yearning," he pits the mocking power of death over against the longing for that which transcends death and is more powerful than death:

> He may not rest with idiot satisfaction,
>   Beneath the cank'ring chain, the curse, the clay,
> But, longing for a wing of sleepless action,
>   Soar for the blessed clime, the enduring day. [15]

It is in the facing of death—which is, as I have said earlier, the ultimate expression of flux—that the hard won proof of something stable, dependable, that still, unchanging center of things that resists the ravages of time and thus resists death, reveals itself. That which is truly of permanent value cannot be found easily, not in those "toys" for which we normally strive:

> How small its worth, how brief its measure,
> How formed to cheat, how little to endure.[16]

In this "there is nought sure but sorrow and transition."[17] But it is in facing this reality that the true *telos* of life comes to light, because

> Man, only, has the privilege to wear
> His crown of thorns—far nobler than the laurel,—
> And wins his immortality from care [18]

Thus, how fitting it is when

> 'Twas in the year when King Uzziah died,
> That, in a vision,—seated in his pride,
> These eyes behold Jehovah on his throne,
> High lifted, and in majesty, alone.[19]

The sentiments expressed by these verses, and the philosophy that makes them more explicit in his public orations, are hardly in keeping with the prevailing dogma of the modern West. It is a countervailing sentiment: one which expresses skepticism regarding all those intellectual predispositions that we usually associate with the European Enlightenment: historical optimism, individualism, autonomous reason, anti-traditonalism—marks of modernity that characterize both his world and ours. More to the point, Simms here rejects a fundamental modern prejudice, one that began, more or less, with Thomas Hobbes, and marks—more than anything else—the true spirit of modernity. Simms uses terms such as permanence, purpose, "rest," stability, eternity, and "place" as the fundamentals of civilization. This contradicts the modern preference for movement, change, dynamism, progress, and revolution, as indicators of health and prosperity.

Between the two is a preference for metaphors. For the ancients the natural state of things is "rest"; for the moderns, "motion." For one, there is a given purpose for things which is the object of their motion; for the other there is no given purpose, only motion and dynamism, which might be brought to bear upon the purposes which human beings shall determine on their own, by their will and their imagination. Between these two metaphors is an abyss, one that separates two worlds, worlds utterly different, that bear the possibility of quite different cultures and produce in time different sorts of human beings. For the very notion of humanity and the human being's relationship to change and permanence expressed by Thomas Traherne and John Stuart Mill, for instance, are *very* different. For Traherne, "That any thing may be found to be an infinit Treasure, its Place must be found in Eernity, and in Gods Esteem. For as there is a Time, so there is a Place for all Things. Evry thing in its Place is Admirable Deep and Glorious: out of its Place like a Wandering Bird, is Desolat and Good for Nothing."[20] A very different idea of human relations within a changing world is found when Mill writes the following in his famous and influential work, *On Liberty:* "[U]ncontrolled freedom of action . . . requires that those who have become bound to one another, in things which concern no third party, should be able to release one another from the engagement: and even without such voluntary release, there are perhaps no contracts or engagements, except those which involve money or money's worth, of which one can venture to say that there ought to be no liberty whatever of retraction. . . . and the most important of these engagements, marriage . . . should require nothing more than the declared will of either party to dissolve."[21]

What has happened in modern thought, however, is that we have attempted to do without the notion of a goal as something that is a given point of reference,[22] what Aristotle would call a "final cause." The idea of a final cause has faded away. The world is explained by material causes (that out of which something is made) and efficient causes (that by which something is made), but not final cause (that for the sake of which something is made). Ever since Hobbes, the idea of *final* cause as indeed a *cause* has been doubted, or at least neglected.

This same idea is often articulated in terms of "motion" and "change." The biblical idea of "rest" contains within it the assumption that the motion of people and things and events anticipates a time of "rest," that is, a time in which their motion is complete, will find its end. It is a way of conceptualizing that things and people have a purpose. Augustine's famous line about his own restless life in his *Confessions* reflected this strong biblical sentiment. This sort of metaphor makes sense in a world that believes things exist, they are "set in motion," for a purpose. In that world, the language of purposefulness, moral responsibility, and moral choice comes naturally.

Hobbes was elated, however, when he thought he had "discovered" a new principle in his encounter with Galileo. The natural state of things is not "rest" but "motion"—all things are in motion, and this, not rest, marks the nature of the world and all things and people in it. This concept, as Hobbes realized, had profound political implications. If *rest* is not the natural state of things, and motion is, then there are no given purposes toward which the world or we move. The nature of things is not *given* and *discoverable*, or it is not something the true nature of which must be *revealed* to us, as Western thinkers from Aristotle to Thomas Aquinas assumed, but it is subject always to change. And if subject to change, it is malleable; and if malleable then the world is essentially unstable. In that case, any order that exists, exists because of the action of human beings upon things. Order is a product of the human will. It is something we make, not something we find and participate in. As Thomas Spragens put it in his *The Politics of Motion*, a book on the thought of Thomas Hobbes, "A world of 'restless' motion which has no *telos* contained restless men who had no *summum bonum*."[23]

The charcteristic feature of modern thought is this change in orientation. Hobbes' "discovery" that all things are in motion and that there is no such thing as a state of "rest" toward which all things move is almost laughable in its apparent naïveté. One wonders if Hobbes is faking an inability to comprehend subtlety, or if he is resorting purposefully to a kind of primitive adoption of literal language. In either event, he takes the metaphor of "rest" as a description of physical destiny. But the seriousness of his modern change of orientation is nevertheless real. If things have purpose—that is, they come to rest, have a destiny—then human beings have a theoretical task before them: they must come to *understand* in order to *act*. But if things have no inherent purpose, and there is no "givenness," and no meaning in using the term "Good" besides what we voluntarily ascribe to it, then our attempts to understand might be considered as tactics in the strategy of coping with the world, but the essential thing is not to understand but to act. And this is what is characteristic of modernity: the shift from the intellect (as a means of understanding the world) to the will (as a means of changing the world).

It is this strong modern predisposition that Simms encountered and challenged in his poetry and his criticism. We are tempted to think that the difficulties Simms encountered in the late nineteenth century were merely products of the historical events of a few decades in American history. Perhaps the truth of it is that the deeply rooted resistance that he encountered was caused by a world that had drunk deeply at the fountain of modernity. And perhaps only now—in the early twenty-first century—when the bitter dregs of modernity are beginning to affect us, and when the boastful claims of the Enlightenment no longer enchant us so, can we fully appreciate the wisdom of Charleston's greatest man of letters.

The Shape of Moral Communities

Can communities be guided and shaped by moral purposes? Only if persons within those communities are trained to see the world as purposefully made, and their lives as participation in a greater calling. This is the significance of the idea of "rest" and the idea of "calling" as opposed to the notion of perpetual whirl as the description of reality. If motion is simply motion and there is no purpose in any motion, then the world itself is without any possible moral structure and our lives have no moral existence in which to participate. But if the movement of things tends toward something meaningful—that is to say, if any event has purpose—then our personal lives and our life together, in family and in community, necessarily relates to that purpose.

What a difference it makes in the way we see the world if, on the one hand, we think of motion as Hobbes did, as simply the change of place—and if we see place, as he did, as a mere geometric abstraction, rather than, as Aristotle did, an irreducible point in reality with its own character. If we see motion, on the other hand, as those from Aristotle to Aquinas saw it, as fulfilling an "end" and as answering to a "final cause," then we have a very different feeling about the world. For Hobbes, motion means that things necessarily change and that the point of human action is to shape those changes. For the classic view of motion, change always portends something beyond itself: for it to have meaning, it does not necessarily need to be guided by the human hand. In fact, by far the greater part of motion is unguided by the human hand. This is why Herbert Butterfield said that "a universe constructed on the mechanics of Aristotle had the door half-way open for the spirits already."[24]

Either life, and the world in which we live, has purpose, or it does not. Most of the modern age has been an attempt to say that although there is no one to assign the world its purpose; we can wrest that purpose out of existence, or we can shape it to our own designs. Yet such programs have proven again and again to be remarkably unsatisfying. And we continually live as if it mattered if life is purposeful or not. If it is, then in one shape or another, we describe and understand our existence as lived out in response to a "vocation," a call to some purpose. It is not necessary that we know what that purpose is, and what character it will ultimately take on. What is very necessary, however, is that there is in fact a purpose to which my life, even in tenuous unsure steps, is seeking to respond.

If life itself is seen as bearing that moral purpose, and if we train ourselves and our young to view the world in that fashion, as a place in which the hardships, the suffering, and the uncertainties are but stations on the way to that for which each of us is cast into the world, and for which we are called to some high purpose, then we shall also have communities shaped by these humane and generous expectations. If we continue, on the other hand, to train ourselves that life is built of the internal drive to exert our several wills upon the world, then the result is, naturally, different. Then we shall continue to find that communities become the arena in which competing wills are brought into constant conflict, and those who are able to marshal resources to "organize" life to fulfill their design, are the only possible prevailing order. And often we will be quite willing to see that happen, since it will be a relief from the promise of continual confict of interests.

Yet there is a better way. And, as the Apostle Paul said, it is the way of love. Communities can also be built around those common values and needs that draw us together out of a common longing, rather than what drives us together out of a common fear.

12

The Return to Community

I N "A WEDDING SERMON FROM A PRISON CELL," Dietrich Bonhoeffer said that it is marriage which sustains love, not love that sustains marriage. As was often the case with this young theologian, who witnessed his country and civilization and then his own freedom become captive to the political idolatry of the time, he cut quickly to the very heart of the problem. Whether in the marriage of two people or the bonds that hold the larger society together, if there is nothing—or no one—greater than frail human intentions to guarantee that bond, then the association, no matter how cherished and privileged at the moment, slips sooner or later into oblivion. P.T. Forsyth stated the case memorably when he wrote, "If within us we find nothing over us we succumb to what is around us."[1]

These bonds of society, while they may be elective in the sense that we enter into them freely (as in marriage, or as in membership in the church) and they may be temporal in that we are born into them (as in a family or a nation), but they are also bonds placed upon us from the outside and as a necessary covenant that endures. As Bonhoeffer says of the wedding vows, "God adds his 'Yes' to your 'Yes.'" If

they do not endure beyond this life, at least the issue of their endur-
ance in life has a bearing upon an eternal destiny. The wedding vows
in the Book of Common Prayer end with a benediction pronounced
upon the couple imploring that they "may so live together in this life,
that in the world to come [they] may have life everlasting."

The point is that, in a real sense, these bonds are not simply
chosen. There is instead a greater stratagem, one of divine initiative, that is at work here. It is paradoxical in the same sense that the
Apostle Paul's words are paradoxical when he says "work out your own
salvation with fear and trembling" (as seen from the temporal and
human side) "for it is God who is at work in you, enabling you both
to will and to work for his good pleasure."[2] In the larger sense, then,
we have not merely chosen these bonds: *It is we who are chosen.* "In
his unfathomable condescension," Bonhoeffer wrote, "God does add
his 'Yes' to yours," but what this means is that "he makes you at the
same time instruments of his will and purpose."[3] Not instruments, in
this sense, *against* your will, but precisely *with* your will. The vision
nurtured by a healthy society is one that includes the possibility, even
the necessity at times, that we who are chosen are in this particular way honored and made fortunate by the calling that is laid upon
us. Our good fortune, and our true destiny, does not lie in severing
these bonds that bind individuals and communities together, but in
outgrowing their necessity. As Boethius said of the lordship of God,
contemplating his own destiny from inside a prison cell, "To be guided
by his reins, to obey his just commands is perfect freedom."[4]

The bonds of community

In recent days much has been said of these "bonds," these sentiments
that are as difficult to define as they are intuitively certain to be necessary to the very existence of a community. René Girard, of Stanford
University, is one who has illuminated the sources of community life

in the effects of imitation or mimesis, and in the contagion of mimetic desires. The following is a brief explanation of his insights.

Everyone is familiar with the transmission of new desires, desires not rooted in physical necessity, such as clothing styles and the size of housing, throughout society. We learn these desires through the imitation of others. Through this contagion of desires our wants are usually not purely personal and individual, but affect groups of people and move people in a common direction. Yet this contagion of mimetic desires, says Girard, gives rise to "scandal" or a "stumbling block" (from the New Testament *scandalon* for "stumbling block"); for, since many desire the same, or almost the same, things, the scarcity of goods in the world—whether those goods be material, like automobiles, or psychological, like fame and esteem—leads to competition for those good things. Thus, what might initially have drawn us together in our common desires ends in drawing us into conflict because they are competing desires. We are not only models for one another in these desires, but also "stumbling blocks" for each other.

The contagion creates multiple stumbling blocks, increasing tension, uncertainty in relations, and the desperate need to clarify the situation, so that society is not paralyzed by its uncertainty and fear. It comes as both a shock and relief to find that there is an enemy upon which to focus one's animosity. It is a shock because the threat appears to be formidable in every sense. But it is a relief in that definite action is called for and becomes possible. When Europe was wracked by spreading plague in the fourteenth century, the doubt, uncertainty, and sense of imminent threat seemed overwhelming. The accusation that the Jews of Europe were poisoning the wells was outlandish, unbelievable even in that pre-scientific period. The news came, however, as a relief. The plague and its accompanying terrors overwhelmed people with the thought that nothing could be done; yet if the Jews were responsible (as unlikely as that was) that meant at least that certain action could be taken in response. The problem was reduced to the size of something that could be handled by a murderous crowd of burgers. Mimetic contagion rises to the occasion, ending in violence and the satisfaction that at least some action could be taken in the defense of the city.

The violent solution must be carefully focused on those who cannot immediately or effectively strike back. They are different, unrelated to the larger society, and unable to effectively defend themselves. This focus allows the newly reborn community—that a moment before lived in tension with each at the throat of the other—to coalesce in fellowship and warm fellow feeling, for their common enemy has made them once again discover their kinship and the possibility of communal action. The crisis that threatened to destroy the community has led to the rebirth of community, a rebirth founded upon a violent action—as Girard would say, upon a founding murder that is later remembered through myth, or remembered historically as the execution of real malefactors.

These are "*Les Choses cachées depuis la fondation du monde*," things hidden from the foundation of the world, to use one of Girard's early titles. All political entities depend upon this "scapegoat mechanism" as a means of ensuring and strengthening their cohesion and their cooperative life together. This rather remarkable view of the foundation of political life is also the view expressed in the Bible, as Girard, a textual critic, says a close reading of the gospels will reveal. While Jesus preferred the language of "scandalon," his disciples habitually prefer the reference to Satan, the "accuser," in order to articulate the same principle. At times the two terms appear together. For instance, at Caesarea Philippi, Jesus had just affirmed Peter's recognition of him as the Messiah, a term normally associated with political office or kingship. Then Jesus predicts his own arrest and crucifixion, a prediction that appears to Peter as the denial of his triumphant accession to the throne. Peter rejects this prediction. Jesus then says, "Get thee behind me Satan [accuser, enemy], for you are an offence [actually *skandalon*, stumbling block] to me."[5] In Matthew's passage on the temptation of Jesus, it is said of the devil that he took Jesus to a very high mountain and tempted him by the offer of "all the kingdoms of the world and their splendor" in exchange for Jesus' worship of him. It is instructive that, unless the line was meant to portray the devil as claiming what is patently not so, the implication is that these "kingdoms" belonged to the devil, which would be illustrative of a consistent New Testament theme.[6] In Luke, the text reads, "To you I will give . . . all this authority; for it has been given over to me, and I give it to anyone I please."[7] Equally important are the words that follow in reply to the temptation in Matthew. "Away with you, Satan [*Hupagé . . . Satana*]!" are the very words found in only one other context: when Jesus silences Peter for insisting on a political understanding of the messianic office.[8]

After reflecting on many of these juxtapositions of political power and the role of the devil or Satan, Jacques Ellul says that "the first Christian generation was globally hostile to political power and regarded it as bad no matter what its orientation or constitutional structures."[9] Furthermore, "we may say that among Jesus' immediate followers and in the first Christian generation political authorities—what we call the state—belonged to the devil and those who held power received it from him. We have to remember this when we study the trial of Jesus."[10] Ellul finds another interesting aspect in the temptation passages with regard to the use of "devil" rather than "Satan" as the primary reference to Jesus' adversary. It is not accidental that the root of this name is the "divider." Government and state are not the sources of society, or of the unity of people, but rather the sources of division and strife. As we have already seen, without reference to an over-againstness that is suggested in political allegiances, there is no political unity as we know it.

Girard makes an even broader point. This animosity is the truth behind social entities of many kinds, including that of the state, but not always confined to it. In a word, the warm, fellow-feeling and the enduring consanguinity of a community depends, more often than we would like to think, on the strength of an animosity and on the murderous intentions of human association. The mentality at the heart of every secure, vibrant nation is that of a lynch-mob. We have only to observe the joy and spirit of patriotism that wells up in a modern nation at a time of war to be partly convinced of that. Using the language of the Gospels, Girard says that "Satan is the principle of every kingdom."[11]

Girard also shows, however, how the gospel has worked as an agent to unravel this Satanic dimension in community life. For the gospel tells the story of the victim, just as the former myths and founding stories tell that kind of story. In the latter, the victim is inevitably considered guilty of the crime he is punished for. It is that guilt that justifies the violence that generates community. By keeping the focus directed at the guilt of the victim, it is easier to divert attention from the lynch-mob mentality of the larger society. The gospel, however, is a subversive story. It tells of a victim, but *from the point of view of the victim*. In this case, one sees clearly the innocence of the victim and the bellicose injustice of the crowd. Because of this story, the evil secret of social cohesion has been uncovered. No longer—since this story has been believed—do people so naively accept the idea of society's unfailing verdict upon its scapegoats. Nor do citizens as easily believe in the victim's guilt.

This does not mean that scapegoating does not work; it only means that, to the extent that this story of the crucifixion of Jesus has worked its way into our minds, the old mechanism has been weakened. The device is still there, as much of a temptation as before, only it is necessary for it to be all the more subtle and cleverly disguised.

Something here is unleashed upon society. The mechanism of social cohesion, relied upon for ages, has lost its full reliability and the life of society itself is threatened along with its (unjust) basis. It is more and more conceived that victims *just might not deserve* their suffering as victims.

This reversal is so powerful, in fact, that now the role of victims can itself be exploited in a way that increases power for some newly emerging alliances armed to avenge the victims and to carry fire and sword against their traditional oppressors. Sometimes these oppressors are real; sometimes they are not. The oppressors take the place of the victims in that they, like the victims, may or may not be legitimately accused. The scapegoat mechanism identified by Girard, working by virtue of mimetic contagion or the spreading imitation of the desires for justice, is never fully defeated, nor fully satisfied: "He goes about to and fro seeking whom he might devour." This scapegoat mechanism transforms itself into ever newer incarnations of the same desire. The liberation movements that have sprung since the French Revolution have never flagged in their inventiveness of clever cases against new victims. These new victims are the church, the traditional family, the institutions of law and commerce and agriculture that have not joined in the cry for empire. It is the cry against all of the "tender bonds" that held society together, the cry that makes all equal, and therefore interchangeable, and therefore the same.[12] The loosening of bonds is called Freedom.

It is not coincidental, as Girard notes, that the "death of Jesus is ultimately decided not by the cry of "crucify him" but rather by "free Barabbas" (Matt. 27:21; Mark 15:11; Luke 23:18). By the same token, it is ironic, but surely not unexpected, that just as earlier societies would cry for "justice" against a malefactor, the modern cry would call for "liberation" against the oppressor—against all the traditional figures of authority, the Priest, the Male, the Father, the family, and the church. The instrument of this liberation has often been seen as the state, though it is the most practiced and capable of oppressors. This is not to say that the state does not have its legitimate role to play; but since it is the most obvious target of the unraveling that began with the gospel, it has had to be clever enough to side with the most common victims in order to continue its exploitation of new victims at a higher level. In effect, it has made the old-time oppressors take their turn as victims, while the state remains hidden behind a curtain called "Freedom."

The imitation of Christ

For the most part, Girard is content to show how the gospel of Christ unveils and exposes, thus subverting, the device of scapegoating. He hints at a new dispensation when he speaks of how the gospel announces the unleashing of the Paraclete, the Holy Spirit. Here we see that the role of Jesus, who "came into the world not to convict the world," is continued in the life of God working in and through followers and imitators of Christ. For Christ is a *parakletos*—that is, a defender, which is the opposite of Satan, whose name means accuser. And the Holy Spirit is "*allon parakleton*," that is, "another defender" *like* Christ (rather than *heteron parakleton*, meaning another, different from). So the role of Jesus was to defend by giving freely of himself for the sake of others. The role clearly differs from the mimetic contagion of those who accuse their victims out of fear and self-defense.

Now I wish to suggest how one might go beyond this hint of an insight. To extrapolate from this pointis not difficult. For it is well laid out for us in the texts and the teachings of the early church. Here we find the basis of an intentionally new community, one based not on fear and self-preservation, but on self-giving in the form of a certain openness to God and a self-forgetfulness that we have learned to call "faith."

To trace what has happened in two thousand years to the idea of imitation in the church—principally the imitation of Christ and through him the imitation of God—would take more space than I have here. Perhaps it is enough to say that modernity, with its preference for "power" or "control," lost the capacity for understanding participation in the sense of a holistic *following* of a *way*. As a result,

Christians can only with difficulty hold on to the true and valid ideas of either doctrine or morality.

Girard's emphasis on the power of imitation is instructive. Everything about the life of a society is learned through imitation. Language is learned by imitating sounds and gestures even before the meaning of those sounds can be known. We learn manners, social ritual, facial expression, a sense of deference, honor, piety, courage, and kindness through imitating those qualities in those who serve as models for us. First, we admire or cherish the object of our attention, a parent, an older friend, a teacher, a coach, even at times a celebrated public figure. From admiration we move to desire, desiring those characteristics that we would emulate, and that desire is contagious; it affects also the desires of others. In this corporate way, social groups move toward the emulation of language, gesture, dress, manners, and even the most subtle of personal qualities.

Imitation is holistic rather than partial. It can, and often does, involve not only speech, but also the body, and that almost indefinable aspect we refer to as "attitude." Focus, attention, energy, tension, humor—these are limited and to some extent governed by genetic predisposition; but they are also, in large degree, stimulated by imitation. The senses of humor exhibited in various regions of the world, for instance, are different, but quite consistent in the region. This is certainly the case in the South, where I live. In four important areas—language, food, humor, and religious practices—there are broad areas of commonality held by Southerners both black and white. This is due to the power of imitation which has flowed all these years in both directions.

Memorization is also imitation, but it is partial. Reasoning also is partial. The modern world was convinced that the world would be governed by "mind" over matter, yet the mind itself, we must admit, is governed mainly by the power and the contagion of imitation within society.

It is no wonder that the very idea of imitation is in eclipse in our times. Ever since the Enlightenment, the emphasis has been upon the individual. Though human nature does not change, and we are as subject to the powers of imitation as ever, we are more likely to hear the advice to "think for yourself," "do not be like others—be yourself," "don't imitate others: instead follow your own lights." Originality is valued; imitation is devalued and made to seem even shameful. We are mildly shocked by the Apostle Paul when he says, "For you yourselves know how you ought to imitate us" (2 Thess. 3: 7) or when he recalls the way he worked among the Thessalonians "in order to give you an example to imitate" (2 Thess. 3:9).

There are two ways that the way of imitation was encouraged in the emerging church of the earliest centuries. First, through the teachings of Jesus and his apostles; and second, through the tradition of building up the church through the intentional cultivation of Christian lives through imitation.

The teachings of Jesus and the apostles

The first way emphasized a new way, a way that transcended the way of violence and domination. Dominating, and therefore violent, power is the method of order in a fallen world. That is clearly the view of the New Testament, which presents Jesus Christ as one who gives up his life, is crushed by the dominating powers of the day, and yet triumphs in a way that is unexpected. By his example, others are called to a life of self-giving, which is the opposite of domination. "The kings of this world have power over their people," Jesus explained to his disciples, "and the rulers are called 'Friends of the People.' But this is not the way it is with you; rather, the greatest one among you must be like the youngest, and the leader must be like the servant. . . . I am among you as one who serves."[13]

Three points must be made here. First, violent and dominating power is of the warp and woof of a fallen order, but this does not mean that it can be abandoned. Indeed, insofar as it exercises power, it only does so as God ordains it; and while its method is not what God calls forth in this redemptive work of Christ, it must be honored for its role in restraining a worse tyranny yet. As long as the old order of the fallen world exists, the two will stand side by side, one restraining a worse evil, and the other leavening the world with a positive good. Second, violent and dominating power, even when it does not reveal its fangs and poses as a "Friend of the People" must be recognized for what it is: a penultimate measure, not the ultimate cure for evil. Christians, and through them others, must learn to tolerate, tame, and regulate it, while fearing its potential for evil. On the other hand, they must learn to love and give themselves over to God, as servants. Third, the teachings of Jesus do not counsel the abandonment of hierarchy, as some tend to read this, as if he were preaching a pristine egalitarian democracy. The hierarchy is clearly still there. Yet it is presented as irony and as paradox, as so much is in the Christian vision of life. For the one who is greatest will be "like the youngest," and the one who will lead is the one who serves all the rest. Jesus is the example: Remember, he said, that the master is thought to be the one who sits at table ready to be served "yet I am among you as one who serves." So rather than denying the hierarchy, he always presents it as irony. After washing his disciples' feet, he says, "Do you know what I have done to you? You call me Teacher [Rabbi or Master] and Lord—*and you are right, for that is what I am.* So if I, your Lord and Teacher, have washed your feet, you ought also to wash one another's feet."[14]

Paul addresses the party spirit and divisions in the Corinthian church. The cure for this loss of community is the proper imitation of those who can be trusted, those who are themselves virtuosos in the imitation of Christ: "I appeal to you, then, be imitators of me." Furthermore, Paul says, "For this reason I sent you Timothy, who is my beloved and faithful child in the Lord, to remind you of my ways in Christ Jesus."[15] In doing this, the followers of Christ are "imitators of God."[16] What it means to be an imitator of God, furthermore, is a new habit of life. Rather than imitating the desires of others in order to gain what they also wish to gain, it is an imitation of precisely the opposite motivation: "Therefore be imitators of God . . . live in love, as Christ loved us and gave himself up for us, a fragrant offering and sacrifice to God."[17] The members of the Christ-imitating community are attentive to a new pattern. Rather than a pattern of self-serving, it is a pattern of serving, giving to, and loving others.

This is a touchstone for understanding the universe itself. The new community responds to a world that reveals the abundant generosity of the One who created and sustains it. The Incarnation is a disclosure of a central fact, that the universe and all of mankind were made for this. Thus the community is formed as participation in this founding and sustaining generosity; not only that, but in anticipation of the fulfillment of all things in this same spirit of mutual giving. Just as the natural community, as Girard found, gains its unity on the basis of mimesis whose end is murder; this new community gains its unity on the basis of the mimetic rivalry of giving. "Outdo one another in good works," writes Paul. "Count others as better than your self."

The fledgling church became illustrative of this principle. Paul writes to the Ephesians about the unity of Jews and Gentiles in Christ: "For he is our peace in his flesh he has made both groups into one and has broken down the divided wall, that is, the hostility between us" (Ephesians 2:14). Paul speaks of hostility between Jews and Gentiles which certainly existed in his own day, and the intensity of their mutual hostility would come to be seen in the violent eruptions of the Jewish Wars a short time later. And this kind of hostility has erupted with particular virulence and with massive bloodshed in the pogroms, the mob actions, and ideological "final solutions" of later times right down to the twentieth century. But Paul's words can be taken as instructive with regard to all ethnic distinctions and all kinds of national rivalries. And even further, it can be taken as illustrative of the fact that any important distinction is potentially a source of hostility.

But if these groups are " in Christ" (a phrase Paul uses liberally especially in Ephesians), then that which formally was the occasion for "dividing walls" (as in the temple) and an occasion for hostility and suspicion becomes now the very way the oneness of new larger association is expressed. The diversity contributes now to a new identity and a new oneness. For those who formerly were at one another's throats because of their differences are now able to see those same differences as gifts.

Those in Christ are "one" in that they receive differences as gifts in the overall unity. They are not "the same" in the sense of a democratic leveling that instinctively fears that differences will inspire envy or suspicion. But they are one in that they all have a transcendent loyalty. They are each called to a higher destiny, and that is altogether different from finding unity in a lower common denominator. That is why it is frequently observed that the gospel calls us to an equality that levels us "up" and is not strongly related to the civil idea of equality that looks to the minimal rights and desires of citizens.

Therefore, Paul begs the Ephesians to lead lives worthy of this high calling, "with all humility and gentleness, with patience, bearing with one another in love." There are words that call for looking to one another with gratitude, not protecting one's own interests, so that the whole body with the full power of the will can "maintain the unity of the Spirit in the bond of peace," thus expressing the reality of "one body and one Spirit . . . one Lord, one faith, one baptism, one God and Father of all, who is above all and through all and in all" (4:2-5).

The differences within the church then are transformed into gifts (v. 11), while in the fallen world they are the sources of envy, fear, power over others, and conflict, giving occasion for "every kind of doctrine" to justify evil, "trickery" to gain advantage over others along with "craftiness and deceitful scheming"(v. 14). The body unified in Christ is a body in which each distinctive part is "working properly" and "promotes the body's growth in building itself up in love" (v. 16).

Early Christianity and the unity of the body

The issue of unity or community continued to be addressed by the early church, in a manner consistent with the understanding of its founding. Among the very early writings known as the *Apostolic Fathers* the issue of unity in the church emerges as a major concern. One of those writings, *First Clement*, written about 95 or 96 AD, makes the point in a way that mirrors the analysis of René Girard. That which begins a community's downward spiral, Clement argues, is jealousy and envy that leads to murder, violence, and corruption. He cites from the Bible a number of cases that illustrate his point, but which also illustrate Girard's idea of mimetic contagion leading to collective violence: Josephs brothers turning against Joseph, Jacob's in-laws persecuting Jacob, Moses' forced flight from Egypt, David's persecution by Saul and his narrow escape from murder. He turns to examples from his own day: the "good Apostles" Peter and Paul, who were persecuted and killed. Jealousy was the root of these deeds: "Jealousy and strife have overthrown great cities and uprooted great nations."[18]

Clement turns immediately to the church's response to these discordant and disruptive effects of mimesis. He understands that jealousy and envy are products of mimetic desire. And the contagious effect of that desire leads to collective violence and murder. In the Christian community, however, one should observe the effects of a wholly constructive and life-giving form of that same desire. To desire not the good effects, or the good fortune observed in others, but to desire the root of human goodness in virtue leads to a mimetic contagion of a different sort. It is in those who are humble, rather than arrogant, that a different kind of unity can be found, not a unity for the sake of warring against others, but a unity for the sake of peace and harmony: "Therefore let us unite with those who devoutly practice peace, and not with those who hypocritically wish for peace." He describes the kind of unifying humility that is found in the words of Isaiah, the Psalms, and then speaks of Jesus himself.

Then he counsels: "You see, dear friends, the kind of pattern that has been given to us; for if the Lord so humbled himself, what should we do?" It is the pattern, learned by imitation, that creates "harmony with intentness of heart."[19]

Thus the church itself is an imitative community, one devoted to learning the pattern of life found in Christ and practiced by those in the church. They pattern their lives after Christ in the confidence that Jesus Christ is the true pattern of God the Father. Some are more mature in this practice than others; some have warranted the judgment that they are "virtuosos" in the faithful imitation of Christ. Thus the reason for the bishop—the overseer—is to provide such an example that others can follow. To say "without a Bishop there is no Church" is hardly a political statement in the ordinary sense of gaining or promoting privilege and rank: it was the common sense observation that since the church forms itself in the imitation of Christ, if there is no authentic and trustworthy exemplar, there is no church. The letters of Ignatius are especially strong on this point. "Do nothing without the bishop," he writes. "Love unity. Flee from divisions. Become imitators of Jesus Christ, just as he is of his Father."[20]

The mimetic pattern flows from God. It continues into the life, speech, thought, practice, of every believer. Just as any culture is constructed by virtue of imitation, so this redemptive fellowship is also formed in that way. Ignatius wrote to the Magnesians, "Therefore as the Lord did nothing without the Father, either by himself or through the apostles (for he was united with him), so you must not do anything without the bishop and the presbyters." In this way a grand unity of the body is formed, with a common *telos* that animates the community so that the members can "all run together as to one temple of God, as to one altar, to one Jesus Christ, who came forth from one Father and remained with the One and returned to the One."[21]

This great theme of imitation and unity from Ignatius is found in seven letters, the authenticity of which is not seriously in doubt.[22] Further, they are quite early; it is almost unanimously agreed among

scholars that they date from the period of Emperor Trajan (98-117 AD).
As for those modern commentators who almost habitually see "power and privilege" as the invisible hand that moves all things, we do
not have to rescue Ignatius from the cynicism of a post-Nietszchian
world. The burden of proof, it seems to me, is to explain what every
responsible scholar recognizes about the remarkable circumstances
of these letters. They were undoubtedly written while Ignatius was on
his way to Rome, in the custody of soldiers (whom he refers to as "ten
leopards"[23]), to be put to death. Under such circumstances, even the
most ambitious of worldly political agendas must necessarily appear
trivial, yet it is under just these circumstances that he underlines again
and again the unity of the body and the necessity of the bishop in
this mimetic fellowship. For it is of the essence of the church, as he
expressed it to the Ephesians, that "you are imitators of God." Their
bishop, Onesimus (perhaps the same as the runaway slave that Paul
converted and is the subject of his letter to Philemon), is described
as "a man of inexpressible love" and it is hoped that "all of you will be
like him."[24] To the Ephesians, Ignatius likens the church to a glorious
choir. In doing so, he stamps this whole issue with a certain aesthetic
image that, in itself, embodies the sentiment that was so strongly held
by the early church:

> Thus it is proper for you to act together in harmony with the
> mind of the bishop, as you are in fact doing. For your presbytery,
> which is worthy of its name and worthy of God, is attuned to
> the bishop as strings to a lyre. Therefore in your unanimity and
> harmonious love Jesus Christ is sung. You must join this chorus,
> every one of you, so that by being harmonious in unanimity and
> taking your pitch from God you may sing in unison with one
> voice through Jesus Christ to the Father, in order that he may
> both hear you and, on the basis of what you do well, acknowledge
> that you are members of his Son. It is, therefore, advantageous
> for you to be in perfect unity, in order that you may always have
> a share in God.[25]

The harvest of a vocational theology

Francis Hutcheson was born the same year as Voltaire, 1694. But perhaps no two men might have had so radically different effects upon history. Hutcheson was an Irish born Scot; Voltaire was French and a Parisian. One grew up in a Presbyterian home, the other in a Catholic home. One wrote careful and prolix dissertations on ethics, beauty, and philosophy; the other penned witty satire and popular drama. One was a critic and corrector of John Locke; the other helped to spread the influence of Locke far and wide, ensuring that it would be an enduring philosophy. Both were, at one time or another, attacked for unorthodox views; for Hutcheson, however, orthodox Christian faith was a matter of deep concern; for Voltaire it was a matter of little moment. Voltaire was once known to say of the church: "Those who can make you believe absurdities can make you commit atrocities."

Hutcheson was enough bothered by the skepticism of his student and erstwhile protegé David Hume that he once refused to recommend him for an important academic chair in Edinburgh. Hutcheson stood at the headwaters of the Scottish Enlightenment, influencing such thinkers as Thomas Reid, David Hume, and Adam Smith. Voltaire was buried near Rousseau, his assumed antagonist, but in truth his fellow pilgrim to the new modern age and was the chief publicist of the English and French Enlightenment. Voltaire had occasional, casual love affairs, save for one long cohabitation, and spoke disparagingly of the female gender; Hutcheson was a faithful husband who argued for the equality of women in marriage. Hutcheson is well known to those who know philosophy; Voltaire is well known to all as "the most famous individual in the eighteenth century."[26] Both spent their active lives far away from their places of birth: Hutcheson was professor of moral philosophy at Glasgow, and Voltaire wrote and entertained at Ferney on the Swiss border. But both died in the course of a trip back to their places of birth, Hutcheson to Ireland and Voltaire to Paris.

In the course of things, history moved toward Voltaire rather than Hutcheson. Isaiah Berlin said of Voltaire, "The friend of kings and the implacable enemy of the Roman Church and indeed, of all institutional Christianity, he was the most admired and dreaded writer of the century, and by his unforgettable and deadly mockery did more to undermine the foundations of the established order than any of its other opponents." No one in the West escaped the effects of his pretended "enlightenment." He was undoubtedly "the intellectual and aesthetic dictator of the civilized world of his day" even though he was not "an original philosopher."[27] Under Voltaire's energetic and creative tutelage, the eighteenth century generally adopted the notion that a new age had indeed begun, that old things were being swept away, and that all things could now be considered all over again. Where necessary, they could be entirely replaced. What had for ages been seen as ignoble might now be dusted off and be found useful, even virtuous.

"Envy" is an example. That which was warned against by Clement, saying that it has "overthrown great cities and uprooted great nations," is reconsidered by Voltaire. The vice which, even now, in the studies of René Girard, stands for the disruption of communities through mimetic rivalry, a stumbling block that divides and subdivides society, might be put to new uses in a new society. The ordering of society, from now on would be effected by the free choice of individuals and the command of the state; it would not be encumbered by clericalism, tradition, mystic communion, or the tender bonds of kinship and friendship. A more rational order must emerge: an order without superstition. Envy occurs to Voltaire as the fountain of a multitude of good things.

Following Mandeville in his *Fable of the Bees*, Voltaire agrees that "without envy the arts would be indifferently cultivated, and that Raphael would not have been a great painter if he had not been jealous of Michael Angelo." Perhaps "emulation is only envy kept within the bounds of decency." Of course, Voltaire is forgetting that emulation

can be the desire for the virtue found in another, and that the successful acquisition of virtue by the admiring soul does not deprive its
original possessor in the slightest. Envy, on the other hand, requires
the diminishing of its object even while wishing its own elevation.
In the former there is contagion but no real rivalry; while in the latter, the contagion must necessarily end in rivalry. But then Voltaire's
contemporaries were apt to forgive his lapse in subtle arguments for
the sake of enjoying a humor subtle enough to suggest that, though
Descartes was wrong when he said envy "impels yellow bile" from
the liver and black bile from the spleen, "A certain Voet or Voetius,
a theological scamp, who accused Descartes of atheism, was very
ill with the black bile; but he knew still less than Descartes how his
detestable bile was diffused in his blood."[28] But, then, Voltaire agreed
with Mandeville that ethics is essentially a more subtle expression of
human self-interest.

It is interesting to speculate what might have happened if the West
had followed a different path. For Hutcheson argued from the insight
that the human being is necessarily social. In his view, we are drawn
toward justice and benevolence as we are drawn toward beauty. Ethical
behavior is not some cunning way of doing what is actually in our own
self-interest. It is, at least in some measure, a reflection of the experience of finding a disinterested pleasure in seeing goodness and justice
performed in public life, just as we are repelled by acts of injustice
and cruelty. We are not so much affected by the thought that the same
thing might happen to us—whether just and benevolent, or unjust
and cruel—as we are affected even when knowledge of the act comes
indirectly and has no relation to us whatever. Think, for instance, what
moves an audience at the theatre. Once the hero of the drama goes
to his peaceful home to find his wife and children murdered and his
home set on fire, we are immediately filled with indignation toward
the criminal who did this unspeakable thing. We are drawn into the
drama and are not satisfied until the villain is caught and, even if it
takes a bloody gun battle, justice is served. Only then do we go out of

the movie theatre with the warm glow of satisfaction from an emo-
tionally cathartic experience. Justice, goodness, and beauty are not
inventions of the intellect whereby the selfish interests of individuals
are satisfied. They represent, if only in some partial way, that toward
which we are ultimately drawn. They are a reflection of the human
being's true vocation: that which speaks strongly to our affections,
which, when we answer its call, we identify as love. It is that which
calls upon the resources of the intellect and mobilizes the will.

As great thinkers from Origen to Augustine to Boethius have seen,
we are necessarily impassioned by the very prospect of what is good,
true, and beautiful. Augustine would express it in his *Confessions*,
in which he saw every human motivation, even those that were directed toward evil, as an attempt to answer to that deep call to know
God and to enjoy him. Yet it is a call that does not isolate us from
the world, but rather embraces the world and all who are in it. The
call is always a social and communal one. We enjoy God only in the
community of others. Even our solitude is good only as it is in some
sense done for the sake of others and then allows us to return to a
community of loved ones with fresh resources and thus fresh gifts
for the community.

The contemplation of what has happened in the course of recent
times induces us to think what might happen if the sentiment of vocation is recovered. Of course, to recover such a perception of life
means nothing less than to recover the spiritual dimension of life in
the form of traditional theism. This was made available for the world
at large only through Christianity, though Christianity, it must be
remembered, was made available to the world only through Judaism.
The idea, therefore, is not foreign to Judaism; indeed, it comes out of
Judaism. But it is through Christianity that the world first learned the
notion that all things can be gathered up in the eternal purposes of
God, that many very *different* things find their unity in a world created
and redeemed by the one God. It is likely that it is only there that such
a persuasive voice will once again be heard. In fact, through the recent

writings of Philip Jenkins we can see just such an experience is being communicated worldwide, so that it is among the growing populations of Asia, Africa, and South America that the world is recovering the strength of Christianity in the full vitality of its orthodox forms.

What, then, might we expect from the reintroduction of orthodox (small "o") Christianity, and the gradual, if not precipitous, abandonment of the secular road down which the world, and especially the West, has been persuaded to travel ever since Bacon, Hobbes, and their contemporaries. Three features of this recovery stand out.

First, the sense of divine vocation is communal in a way that Girard and Hutcheson, as well as Clement and Ignatius, have suggested to us. Girard saw the effects of a mimetic contagion, one that breaks down with the appearance of *skandeloi*, stumbling blocks; that is, with the appearance of conflicting interests arising from competing desires, or mimetic rivalry. The early Christians, following the teachings of Jesus and Paul, had discovered a kind of contagious desire that does *not* break down in unresolvable rivalry and conflict. Benevolence, born of love and generosity, is also (as Hutcheson pointed out) an object of desire. And because it is unlimited it is also never subject to rivalry. The generosity, benevolence, forgiveness, and mercy of God finds representatives in the community of disciples (imitators of Christ, whose own benevolence is mediated through virtuosos in the community). Such a way of life provokes desire in the larger society, further stimulus for imitation. Thus the community—which otherwise could only operate on the primordial principal of rivalry—becomes open in principle to the world itself. The harmony of this mutual self-giving portends a greater harmony in what Christians always anticipated as a reign of peace.

Second, the virtues of generosity, kindness, mercy, forgiveness— while never merely natural or easily aquired—are more congenial to this view of life. They are therefore taught, not as graces that jar and fit awkwardly with the larger culture and its public philosophy, or as something that serves as pragmatic oil to grease the machinery of human cooperation, but as integral habits in a community founded on a call to transcend narrow self-interest. This ecumenical and open community is a community based on giving rather than dividing. Its mode is one of giving out of the abundance of life, rather than diving the spoils of conquest. Mutual generosity is the very expression of unity.

Third, distinctions among people and between persons are are an embarrassment to a culture shaped by the market and the acquisition of power. In this cultural environment, we must be persuaded that differences are either meaningless or constitute "the hill on which we must die" in combating the rest of humanity. It is not only a relief, but positively good news, in the light of a vocational understanding of life, that differences are good also. It is true that in a fallen world they are the occasions of distrust, envy, misunderstanding, animosity, and shame. But this comes from the failure to discern that differences are gifts for others, not occasions for animosity. In this they do not isolate us but unite us. Races, genders, language groupings, and the like, are classically points of misunderstanding and conflict. But they also represent ways in which we grasp the world differently, through different cultures and sentiments, through various metaphors and syntax. As such, each of these human differences can be the basis for understanding existence in a valid, albeit partial, way. Thus with our insights, shaded toward different emphases, enjoying and using the world in our slightly different ways, we are enabled to enrich the greater community. While giving expression to what is temporally divided, we begin together to give witness to what is finally united. For the end of all things is the God who calls us, in whom we find rest, by whose one light we find our separate ways toward that city "not made with hands, eternal, in heaven." Those who pilgrim toward that ultimate goal, even while they are separate, and acknowledging that their experiences and ways are distinct, can yet give loving witness to the fact that, in the mystery of God's calling, they are one.

Throughout this work I have returned, at frequent intervals, to a central conviction. Perhaps, at first, it was mere intuition; but in ways, it has served as a "vocation" for this period in my life. Seeking to view this thought from every facet that presented itself to me, over a seasonably long time, the first intuition was sustained, even while it grew more complex, or perhaps gained in a feeling of solidity and weight. The thought is essentially this: Only when members of a community understand life as a response to a large and generous world, created by a great and merciful Providence, will the possibilities of life together become more fully realized. Otherwise, without this spirit infusing and animating a people, existence is reduced to competing forces, clashing at twilight, grasping whatever is left of power, fame, and fortune, before the darkness descends. For then, while the isolation becomes rooted in every human domain, its end is necessarily found in the dust of death. But with this spirit of vocation, this conviction that we are not, after all, our own, but belong to Another, the world opens up, becomes a place for others, and is illuminated by a spreading and abiding hope.

Afterword

James C. Conyers

A. J. Conyers died of cancer on July 18, 2004, a few days after submitting the final manuscript for this book. This afterword is the eulogy delivered by his brother, the Reverend James C. Conyers, on July 22, 2004, at his funeral at the First Baptist Church of Waco, Texas.

THIS IS AN "ODE TO AN ATHLETE DYING YOUNG." It is a portrait of someone at the height of his career. A few weeks ago, Chip told me that he had received an invitation to give a paper at a prestigious symposium at the Vatican next March.

I said to him, "If you go, I'll carry your bags for you."

And he responded, "Oh, you don't have to do that."

And I said, "Being the little brother of the perfect older brother, I have been carrying your baggage all my life, so this will be no different."

When I took our father home with me in May, not a word passed between the three of us, but we knew that this would the last time that my father would see his son. Chip's emaciated appearance was a sign

194

that life was passing away, that death would ultimately, eventually, and inevitably take him. He was, as St. Paul writes of himself in his second letter to Timothy "on the point of being sacrificed, and the time of my departure is at hand. I have fought a good fight, I have finished my course, I have kept the faith" (2 Timothy 4:6-7). My brother lived as a martyr; my brother also died as a martyr. He was a witness in the midst of life of something that is greater than we may see. He fought the good fight, he finished the race, and he kept the faith.

I remember that he gave his life to Christ when he was just eight years old. And from then on he had a vocation that he faithfully followed. He had a vocation as a theologian, as a writer, as a husband, as a father, and as a grandfather. All of these vocations he took as callings from God that he was to fulfill faithfully, and he did.

My brother was an organizer. He was an organizer of words on the page. When we were very young, he wrote and published *The Conyers Family Newspaper*—circulation of four! As we were growing up he was an organizer of people and events in the neighborhood. He organized the neighborhood boys in a junior Olympics. He organized a Family Museum—an eclectic display that many friends and neighbors came to see. He was especially an enthusiastic organizer of his little brother, who was usually less than appreciative of his efforts. But he was also a witness to me, a witness of one walking in the way of the cross, in the way of Christian discipleship. And when I walked away from Christ and from the church for fifteen years as a young adult, he was the one who brought me back.

He has left us all a great witness in his writings. And one thing that probably almost no one in this room has seen is his last book, a powerful book about the theology of vocation, some of which I would like to share. It is called *The Listening Heart*. In the preface, he lays out the thesis of the book, which is a look at the meaning of the Christian theology of vocation. And he writes that here we find an alternative to the centrality of choice. "Choice" is such a sacred word in our secular world! The alternative to the centrality of choice is vocation. He wrote: "For it is a precisely choice, when it is the first word of our vocabulary, that pulls us apart, likewise it is vocation that calls us together." At the end of that book he wrote this:

> Throughout this work I have returned, at frequent intervals, to a central conviction. Perhaps, at first, it was mere intuition; but in ways, it has served as a "vocation" for this period in my life. . . . The thought is essentially this: Only when members of a community understand life as a response to a large and generous world, created by a great and merciful Providence, will the possibilities of life together become more fully realized. Otherwise, without this spirit infusing and animating a people, existence is reduced to competing forces, clashing at twilight, grasping whatever is left of power, fame, and fortune, before the darkness descends. For then, while the isolation becomes rooted in every human domain, its end is necessarily found in the dust of death. But with this spirit of vocation, this conviction that we are not, after all, our own, but belong to Another, the world opens up, becomes a place for others, and is illuminated by a spreading and abiding hope.

My brother died as a martyr. He died pointing for us the way to this spreading and abiding hope of Jesus Christ who is ours and to whom we belong.

Notes

1   The Era of Bloodshed

1   James 4: 1,2 (*Revised Standard Version* of the Bible).
2   This was published along with a series of photographs taken in the late 1920's and early 1930's by Doris Ulmann. The series was published as *The Appalachian Photographs of Doris Ulmann* (Highlands, NC: The Jargon Society, 1971). This book is one of the most fascinating collections of portraits I have ever run across, in part because of the skill of the photographer no doubt, but certainly in part due to the deeply etched character of the people from that region, among whom it was my good fortune to find a wife.

2   Vocation and Community

1   Henri Bergson, *The Two Sources of Morality and Religion* (Garden City, NY: Doubleday, 1954).
2   Exodus 6:12 (NRSV).
3   Jeremiah 11:19 (NRSV).
4   Gerhart Niemeyer, *Within and Above Ourselves: Essays in Political Analysis* (Wilmington, Delaware: Intercollegiate Studies Institute, 1996), 369.
5   Immanuel Kant, "What is Enlightenment?" [1784] in *The Philosophy of*

Kant: Immanuel Kant's Moral and Political Writings, ed. Carl J. Friedrich (New York: The Modern Library, 1993), 145.

6 Ibid., 147.

7 Ibid., 152.

8 Judges 17:6 (RSV).

9 Genesis 1:27 (NRSV).

10 Genesis 1:26 (RSV).

11 Genesis 1:27.

12 With regard to Origen's doctrine of vocation, I have been considerably aided, and in this study am in debt to, the excellent monograph by Fr. José Alviar, *Klesis: The theology of the Christian Vocation According to Origen* (Dublin, Ireland: Four Courts Press, 1993).

13 Alviar, *Klesis*, 27.

14 Genesis 17: 1 (my translation) and 8 (RSV).

15 Ezekiel 33: 20b (RSV). The fuller text is set over against the complaint directed toward their national fate in view of the faithfulness of some: " 'Yet your people say, "The way of the Lord is not just"; when it is their own way that is not just. When the righteous turns from his righteousness, and commits iniquity, he shall die for it. And when the wicked turns from his wickedness, and does what is lawful and right, he shall live by it. Yet you say, "The way of the Lord is not just." O house of Israel, I will judge each of you according to his ways.' " (vv. 17-20).

16 1 Kings 19.

17 Dietrich Bonhoeffer, *The Cost of Discipleship* (New York: The Macmillan Company, 1969), 105-114. He says for instance, "Through the call of Jesus men become individuals. Willy-nilly, they are compelled to decide, and that decision can only be made by themselves. It is no choice of their own that makes them individuals: it is Christ who makes them individuals by calling them. Every man is called separately, and must follow alone. But men are frightened of solitude, and they try to protect themselves from it by merging themselves in the society of their fellowmen and in their material environment. . . . But all this is only a cloak to protect them from having to make a decision." (105).

18 Galatians 3:28 (New American Standard Bible).

19 Robert B. Shaw, *The Call of God: The theme of Vocation in the Poetry of Donne and Herbert* (Cowley Publications, 1981), 5.

20 Romans 1:1,2 (RSV, except for "slave" which I rendered here literally in order to emphasize the arduous nature of the calling).

21 Romans 1:7 (RSV).

22 Romans 15:16 (RSV).

23 I Corinthians 4: 9-13 *passim* (RSV).

24 2 Corinthians 6: 4,5 (RSV).
25 Galatians 6:17 (RSV).
26 Ephesians 2: 5, 10 (RSV).

3   The Broken Image

1 John Calvin, *Institutes*, III, 10,6.
2 See Dietrich Bonhoeffer, *Ethics* (New York: Simon & Schuster, 1995), 250.
3 Bonhoeffer, *Ethics,* 251.
4 Frances A. Yates, *Giordano Bruno and the Hermetic Tradition* (New York: Vintage Books, 1969), 111.
5 Peter Lassman, Irving Velody, and Herminio Martins, eds., *Max Weber's 'Science as a Vocation'* (London: Unwin Hyman, 1989), 22.
6 Ibid., 23.
7 Ibid., 22.
8 Weber, "Science as a Vocation," 22.
9 With regard to the "researcher into culture and the sources of community" I also have in mind that every Christian (and one might easily make an argument for every monotheist in this case, but I happen to be a Christian and a student of theology) is a researcher into culture and the sources of community. This is so inasmuch as every person who, through the teachings and the experience of their own faith, place themselves in the midst of a community practice (culture) and trust in the sources of community (love and justice, issuing in peace) find themselves the brother or sister of a catholic humanity and a participant in (rather than a master of) nature.
10 Eric Voegelin, *Revolution and the New Science*, Volume VI of *History of Political Ideas, and Volume 24* of *The Collected Works of Eric Voegelin* (Columbia and London: University of Missouri Press, 1998), 173.
11 Psalm 98:7,8 (NRSV).
12 Franz Kafka, *Parables and Paradoxes* (New York: Schocken, 1958), 93.

4   The Decline of Vocation

1 In his *History of Political Ideas, Volume II: The Middle Ages to Aquinas* (Volume 20 of *The Collected Works of Eric Voegelin* [University of Missouri Press, 1997]) can be found a profitable study of how "cause" as a political outworking of the warrior-monk began in the middle ages to replace the more holistic notion of the Christian charismatic community, and with this more contemporary result: "The mystic warrior attitude begins to appear again with the rise of spiritual movements

among the people and their organization of combat units on a popular basis .... Marston Moor in 1644 is the symbol of the beginning of a new epoch. The national mass army since the French revolution marks a further step in the revolution insofar as nationalism becomes the spiritual cause.... The revolutionary political associations, *Bünde* or *fasci* from the *Giovane Italia* of Mazzini to the Bolshevik professional revolutionaries, the *fasci* of Mussolini, and the National socialist movement, are the model cases of the modern political soldier united with his comrades by *the spiritual substance of a cause*" [emphasis mine]. (76-77).

2 Albert Camus, *The Rebel: An Essay on Man in Revolt* (New York: Vintage International, 1991), 275.

3 Aristotle, *Politics*, Bk. 1, Ch. 4. The Philosopher goes to some lengths with arguments of this kind in order to establish that the state of the slave is a "natural" one and thus can be defended as just. For instance, "As in the arts which have a definite sphere the workers must have their own proper instrument for the accomplishment of the work, so it is in the management of the household. Now instruments are of various sorts; some are living, others are lifeless; in the rudder, the pilot of a ship has a lifeless, in the look-out man, a living instrument; for in the arts the servant is a kind of instrument." *Politics* trans. by Benjamin Jowett in *Great Books of the Western World* ed. by Robert Maynard Hutchins (Chicago: Encyclopaedia Britannica, 1952), 447.

4 The passages here are taken from a citation of *In Ecclesiastes Homiliae* in Trevor Dennis, "Man Beyond Price: Gregory of Nyssa and Slavery," in *Heaven and Earth: Essex Essays in Theology and Ethics*, edited by Andrew Linzey and Peter Wexler (West Sussex: Churchman Publishing Limited, 1986), 134-137.

5 *Encyclopedia of Religion and Ethics*, edited by James Hastings (Edinburgh: T. & T. Clark, 1920) Vol XI, 608.

6 Elizabeth Fox-Genovese and Eugene D. Genovese, *Fruits of Merchant Capital: Slavery and Bourgeois Property in the Rise and Expansion of Capitalism* (Oxford: Oxford University Press, 1983), vii.

7 David Brion Davis, *Slavery and Human Progress* (Oxford: Oxford University Press, 1984), 76.

8 Ibid.

9 Ibid., 81.

10 Cf. Leviticus 25.

11 Davis, 15-16.

12 Ibid., 14.

13 Cited by Davis, 15; the citation is from Orlando Patterson, *Slavery and Social Death* (Cambridge, MA: Harvard University Press, 1982), 51.

14 Patterson (cited by Davis, 15), 302.
15 Davis, 15.
16 W.T. Sherman: Reply to an Indian at Fort Cobb, I. T., who said "Me good Indian," January 1869.
17 Jürgen Moltmann, *God for a Secular Society* (Minneapolis: Fortress, 1999), 12,13.
18 Ibid., 15.

5 Distraction

1 The essay by Theodore M. Greene, is found in Immanuel Kant, *Religion Within the Limits of Reason Along* (New York: Harper Torchbook, 1960), ix-lxxviii. As of 2001, this edition along with this essay, entitled "The Historical Context and Religious Significance of Kant's *Relgion*," was still in print.
2 Greene, ix.
3 Moltmann, *God for a Secular Society*, 7-8. Emphasis is added.
4 Kant,"What is Enlightenment?", 145.
5 Greene, x.-xi.
6 Johannes Kepler, *The Harmony of the World*, Trans. by E. J. Aiton, A. M. Duncan, J. V. Field (Philadelphia: American Philosophical Society, 1997), 491.
7 *Teaching Christianity: De Doctrina Christiana*, Trans. Edmund Hill, O.P., Part I, Vol 11 of *The Works of Saint Augustine A Translation for the 21st Century*, ed. John E. Rotelle, O.S.A. (Hyde Park, NY: New City Press, 1996), 107-108.
8 Simone Weil, *Gravity and Grace*, Trans. By Arthur Wills (Lincoln: University of Nebraska Press, 1997), 170.

6 Power

1 Luke 22:25,26 (NRSV)
2 1 John 4:18.
3 M. J. Tooley, in his traslation of Bodin's *Six Books of the Commonwealth* (Oxford: Basil Blackwell, no date), writes of Bodin's work, "The resemblance to Machiavelli is too close to be fortuitous. Machiavelli's collected works were published in 1550, and Bodin refers to the *Prince*, the *Discourses on Livy*, and the *History of Florence*, besides basing a chapter [V,v] on the *Art of War*. In the introduction to the *Discourses* he could find the statement that history is the proper study of the statesman because, human nature being constant, men always behave in the same way, and therefore the same sequence of cause and effect is always

repeating itself. One learns by the experience of others. In the *Prince* and the *Discourses* he could see Machiavelli applying this principle by regularly juxtaposing examples of what he was discussing taken first from ancient and then from contemporary history, deducing general conclusions, and so proceeding to frame general maxims. Bodin took over the method but vastly extended the scope. He thought Machiavelli's survey too restricted to allow of conclusions universally valid, and complained that he was very ignorant of many things because he had not read a sufficiency of good books, nor acquainted himself with any peoples but the Italians" (xviii).

4   Bodin, *Six Books of the Commonwealth*, 140.
5   Ibid., 141.
6   Introduction to Bodin, *Six Books of the Commonwealth*, xxxix.
7   Ludivicus J. Diecmann, *De naturalismo* (Leipzig, 1684), 3. Cited in Marion Leathers Daniels Kuntz, ""Religion in the Life of Jean Bodin," and introductory essay to Jean Bodin, *Colloquium of the Seven about Secrets of the Sublime (Colloquium Heptaplomeres de Rerum Sublimium Arcanus Abditis* (Princeton: Princeton University Press, 1975), xxviii.
8   Cited in Kuntz, "Religion in the Life of Jean Bodin," *Colloquium*, xxiii-xxiv.
9   Girard cites E. E. Evans-Pritchard, "Witchcraft," *Africa* 8 (1955), 418-419, in *The Scapegoat*, trans. Yvonne Freccero (Baltimore: The Johns Hopkins University Press, 1986), 53.
10   Girard, *The Scapegoat,* 53.
11   See the last three chapters of *I See Satan Falling Like Lightening* (New York: Orbis Press, 2001).
12   F. H. Anderson, *The Philosophy of Francis Bacon* (Chicago: University of Chicago Press, 1948), 7.
13   Anderson, *Francis Bacon*, 7.
14   Loren Eiseley, *The Man Who Saw Through Time* (New York: Charles Scribner's Sons, 1973), 22,23.
15   Anderson, *Bacon*, 33.
16   In using the term "total critique" here, I am reflecting the insights of the late Gerhart Niemeyer who saw in modern thought a penchant for casting all cultivated life and thought aside and beginning again. It is he who caused me to understand that this is not the most natural way to approach an intellectual or a moral issue. His book that brings this insight into sustained focus is *Between Paradise and Nothingness* (Baton Rouge: LSU Press, 1975).
17   Francis Bacon, "The Refutation of Philosophies," translated by Benjamin Farrington and included in his *Philosophy of Francis Bacon* (Chicago: University of Chicago Press, 1964), 103.

18 "The Refutation of Philosophies," in *Philosophy of Francis Bacon* by Benjamin Farrington, 126.

19 Cited in Anderson, *Bacon*, 11.

20 For instance John Dewey in his Gifford Lectures of 1929, *The Quest for Certainty* and Stephen Toulmin in *Cosmopolis: The Hidden Agenda of Modernity* (Chicago: University of Chicago Press, 1990).

21 A remark of Archimedes quoted by Pappus of Alexandria in his 'Collection' (*Synagoge*, Book VIII, c. A.D. 340 [ed. Hultsch, Berlin 1878,p. 1060]).

22 Robert P. Kraynak, "John Locke: From Absolutism to Toleration," *American Political Science Review* 74 (1980), 54.

23 Ralph Waldo Emerson, "Nature," in *The Oxford Authors: Ralph Waldo Emerson*, edited by Richard Poirier (Oxford and New York: Oxford University Press, 1990), 3.

24 Cited in Benjamin Farrington, *Philosophy of Francis Bacon*, 27.

25 Francis Bacon, *The Masculine Birth of Time*, translated by B. Farrington and included in his *Philosophy of Francis Bacon*, 62.

26 Ibid., 68.

27 René Descartes, *Discourse on the Method of Rightly Conducting the Reason*, in *The Philosophical Works of Descartes*, trans. E.S. Haldane and G.R.T. Ross, revised ed. (Cambridge: Cambridge University Press, 1979), 119.

28 Marion Montgomery, *Possum, and Other Receits for the Recovery of "Southern" Being* (Athens: University of Georgia Press, 1987), 6. He follows this point with a remarkable quotation from Bacon's *New Atlantis*: "'That noblest foundation that ever was upon earth,' he says, meaning his utopian island of 'New Atlantis' 'the knowledge of causes and the secret motion of things; and the enlarging of the bounds of human empire, to the effecting of all things possible.'" At every turn, we find Bacon's interest is revealed more as the increase of power and the pursuit of conquest, rather than science as it was traditionally understood.

29 An excellent study of this development in modern thought, with roots in medieval theological disputes is Amos Funkenstein's *Theology and the Scientific Imagination: from the Middle Ages to the Seventeenth Century* (Princeton, New Jersey: Princeton University Press, 1986). Also this issue is dealt with many times in the writings of Jürgen Moltmann: I would mention particularly *The Trinity and the Kingdom* (1979), and *God for a Secular Society* (1999).

30 *The Oxford Authors: Ralph Waldo Emerson*, 64.

31 Genesis 2:18.

32 "The Letter of Ignatius to the Ephesians," *The Apostolic Fathers*, Second

Edition. Trans. by J. B. Lightfoot and J. R. Harmer, ed. and revised by Michael W. Holmes (Grand Rapids: Baker Book House, 1994), 86,87.

7 *Life Together*

1 For an excellent treatment of "scale" in community, see Donald Livingston's "Dismantling Leviathan" in *Harper's* (May 2002), 13-17.
2 David Gelernter, "Judaism Beyond Words," *Commentary* (May, 2002), 31-32.
3 Romans 10 is the passage referred to here and in the following comments. The translation used here is the Revised Standard Version.
4 Jürgen Moltmann, *The Coming of God* (Minneapolis: Fortress, 1996), 220.
5 Jürgen Moltmann, *God for a Secular Society* (Minneapolis: Fortress, 1999), chapter two.

8 *Attention*

1 "What is a Jew? A Letter to a Minister of Education," in George A. Panichas, ed., *The Simone Weil Reader* (New York: David McKay Company, 1977), 79-81. The editor of this reader, George Panichas, points to the reason she might have been circumspect in the way she approached the topic: "She was careful not to condemn all those working with Vichy. Since the armistace was 'a collective act of cowardice,' she believed that the words 'traitor,' 'coward,' and 'collaborator' should be used guardedly" (introductory note, 79).
2 Quoted in the "Introduction" by Leslie A. Fiedler, to Simone Weil, *Waiting for God* (San francisco: Harper & Row, 1951), 9.
3 Fiedler, 7.
4 Quoted in Panichas, *Reader*, 94.
5 Ibid., xxxix.
6 "Spiritual Autobiography," in Panichas, *Reader*, 15-16.
7 This essay appears in *Waiting for God* (San Frncisco: Harper & Row, 1951), 105-116.
8 Simone Weil, *Waiting*, 106.
9 Ibid.
10 Ibid., 112.
11 Ibid., 107.
12 Ibid., 159.
13 These words reflect Mark 13:13, which appears in the parallel passage to Matthew 24-25.

14 Matthew 25:40 NRSV.

15 Needleman, Jacob, *The Heart of Philosophy* (San Francisco: Harper & Row, 1986), 35.

16 G. K. Chesterton, *Orthodoxy* (Garden City, N.Y., 1959), 131.

17 Walker Percy, "Novel Writing in an Apocalyptic Time" in *Signposts in a Strange Land*, ed. Patrick Samway (New York: Farrar, Straus, and Giroux, 1991), 162.

9   *Tolerance*

1   I have in mind John Dewey's Gifford lectures published as *The Quest for Certainty* (New York: Minton, Balch, & Company, 1929), and Stephen Toulman in *Cosmopolis: the hidden agenda of modernity* (Chicago: University of Chicago Press, 1990).

2   Cited in Donald Livingston, "The Very Idea of Secession," *Social Science and Modern Society*, Vol. 35 (July/August, 1998), 39.

3   John Locke, *A Letter Concerning Toleration* (Buffalo,NY: Prometheus Books, 1990), 18-19.

4   Ibid., 22.

5   As cited in Josef Pieper, *The Silence of St. Thomas*, trans. by John Murray, S.J. and Daniel O'Connor (New York: Pantheon Books, 1957), 4, 5.

6   Thomas Aquinas, *Summa Theologica* in *Introduction to Thomas Aquinas*, ed. Anton Pegis (New York: The Modern Library, 1948), 170-171.

7   Simone Weil, *Gravity and Grace* (Lincoln, Nebraska: University of Nebraska Press, 1997), 106.

8   Henry Chadwick, *The Early Church* (London: Penguin Books, 1993), 77.

9   *Stromata* I:94.

10 Gregory Nazianzen, "Oration on the Holy Lights,"*Nicene and Post-Nicene Fathers, Second Series*, Vil 7 (Peabody, MA: Hendrickson, 1994), 361.

11 Louis Dupré, "The Dialectic of Faith and Atheism in the Eighteenth Century," in <ichael J. Himes and Stephen J. Pope (eds.), *Finding God in All Things: Essays in Honor of Michael J. Buckley, S.J.* (New York: The Crossroad Publishing Company, 1996), 39.

12 St. Basil the Great, *De Spiritu Sanctu*, (XXVI, 61) Trans. by The Rev. Blomfield Jackson, M.A., Vol. 8 of *Nicene and Post-Nicene Fathers*, 38.

13 Augustine, *Confessions* (vii.9), Trans. R.S. Pine-Coffin (London: Penguin, 1961), 145.

14 De Doctr. Christ. ii. 28 in *Nicene and Post-Nicene Fathers*, Vol. 2, 545.

15 De Doctr. Christ. ii. 61 in *Nicene and Post-Nicene Fathers*, Vol. 2, 554.

10   *Tolerance*

1   According to philosopher Edward S. Casey (*Getting Back into Place* [Bloomington: Indiana University Press, 1993], 14) Aristotle "was acutely sensitive to this fundamental point" that place is prior to all things. Prior to his judgment on this matter however was that of the Pythagorean Archytas of Tarentum (428-347 B.C.) who said: "Since everything that is in motion is moved in some place, it is obvious that one has to grant priority to place, in which that which causes motion or is acted upon will be. Perhaps thus it is the first of things, since all existing things are either in place or not without place."

2   Columbia: University of South Carolina Press, 1998.

3   Nathanael Dresser saw this in his essay on Ed Abbey and Wendell Berry ("Cultivating Wilderness: The Place of Land in the Fiction of Ed Abbey and Wendell Berry," *Growth and Change,* Vol. 26 [Summer 1995], 352) when he wrote that "the land is not simply a setting for Abbey and Berry, nor is it an ideal paradise. Rather the land is a virtual character in itself, one with which the humans interact."

4   Richard Wilbur's "Introduction", in Alan Gussow and Richard Wilbur, *A Sense of Place: The Artist and the American Land* (Island Press, 1997).

5   Flannery O'Connor, *Mystery and Manners* (New York: Farrar, Straus & Giroux, 1962), 59.

6   Emphasis mine.

11   *Rest*

1   Thomas A.Spragens, Jr., *The Politics of Motion* (Lexington: University Press of Kentucky, 1973), 53.

2   One of these literary societies to which Simms spoke was the venerated Demosthenian Society, of which I was a member, and at one time president, around 1965.

3   Boethius, *Consolation of Philosophy*, trans. by P.G. Walsh (Oxford: Oxford University Press, 1999), 25.

4   A more traditonal rendering of the passage in *Confessions*, Book I, Chapter 1, and also found in Saint Augustine, *Confessions* , Trans. R.S. Pine-Coffin (London: Penguin Books, 1961), 21.

5   *The Social Principle* (Tuscaloosa, AL, 1843), 15.

6   Ibid., 19.

7   Ibid., 37.

8   Ibid., 36.

9   Ibid., 42.

10 Ibid., 43.

11 *Self-Development* (Milledgeville, 1847), p.40.

12 Ibid., 38.

13 *Sabbath Lyrics*, p. 53.

14 Ibid., 70.

15 Ibid.

16 Ibid., 64.

17 Ibid.

18 Ibid.

19 Ibid., 59.

20 Also there is a remarkable piece by Augustine on the "weight of love": "A body tends by its weight towards the place proper to it—weight does not necessarily tend towards the lowest place but towards its proper place. Fire tends upwards, stone downwards. By their weight they are moved and seek their proper place. Oil poured over water is borne on the surface of the water, water poured over oil sinks below the oil: it is by their weight that they are moved and seek their proper place. Things out of their place are in motion: they come to their place and are at rest. My love is my weight: wherever I go my love is what brings me there."

21 John Stuart Mill, *On Liberty and Other Writings*, ed. Stefan Collini (Cambridge: Cambridge University Press, 1989), 103.

22 Modern thinkers such as John Dewey want to express this as a "fixed" point of reference, as if the adequacy of the idea is totally dependent on the adequacy of a certain metaphor. To say that the "good" is fixed and stable is only an attempt to say that it does not depend upon us, but something that stands over against us—it is *given* and perhaps discoverable, but not invented and the product of artifice.

23 Spragens, *The Politics of Motion*, 205.

24 Cited in Spragens, 59. Herbert Butterfield, *The Origins of Modern Science (New York: Collier, 1962)*, 19.

12   The Return to Community

1 P.T. Forsyth, *The Cure of Souls: An Anthology*, ed. Harry Escott (Grand Rapids, Eerdmans, 1971), 61.

2 Philippians 2: 12, 13 (NRSV).

3 Dietrich Bonhoeffer, *Letters and Papers from Prison* (New York: Touchstone, 1997), 42.

4 Boethius, *The Consolation of Philosophy*, trans., P. G. Walsh (Oxford: Oxford University Press, 1999), 14.

5 Matthew 16:23 (my own translation).

6   Matthew 4:8-9. Of course, not all are convinced of this. One of my professors in seminary remembers driving in a small rural community where he picked up the radio broadcast of a local preacher. This excitable evangelist came upon these lines in Matthew and became so worked up over the very idea that the devil claimed these kingdoms were his to give that, in a sudden outburst, he said, "That devil was a lying son of a bitch—he never owned those kingdoms." Nevertheless, the text seems to consistently associate the devil or Satan with the power by which kingdoms are founded. And here Jacques Ellul (*Anarchy and Christianity* [Grand Rapids: Eerdmans, 1991], 58) writes: "Jesus does not say to the devil: It is not true. You do not have power over kingdoms and states. He does not dispute this claim." If that had been the case, either Matthew or Luke, or both, would have made it clear that this was at issue in Jesus' rejection. Instead, they make the issue Jesus' rejection of the very right to this political authority on the grounds that to accept it would be tantamount to the worship of the devil. Jacques Ellul finds it extraordinary that more has not been made of this connection in the text.

7   Luke 4:6 (NRSV).

8   Matthew 4:10 and Matthew 16:23.

9   Jacques Ellul, *Anarchy and Christianity*, trans by Geoffrey Bromiley (Grand Rapids: Eerdmans, 1991), 59.

10   Ibid. 58.

11   René Girard, *The Scapegoat*, trans. by Yvonne Freccero (Baltimore: Johns Hopkins University Press, 1986), 187.

12   Ibid., 203.

13   Luke 22: 25-27 (TEV).

14   John 13: 12-14 (NRSV). The emphasis is mine.

15   I Corinthians 4: 16,17.

16   Ephesians 5:1.

17   Ephesians 5: 1,2.

18   *The Apostolic Fathers*, trans. by J.B. Lightfoot and J. R. Harmer, ed. and revised by Michael W. Holmes (Grand Rapids: Baker Book House, 1994), 31.

19   *The Apostolic Fathers*, 36, 37, and 47.

20   Ignatius' letter to the Philadelphians, *Apostolic Fathers,* 108.

21   Ignatius' letter to the Magnesians, *Apostolic Fathers*, 95.

22   Of the seven letters, six are addressed to churches—Ephesians, Magnesians, Trallians, Romans, Philadelphians, Smyrnaeans—and one to his fellow bishop Polycarp.

23   Ignatius, the Roman letter, *Apostolic Fathers*, 104.

24   Ignatius, To the Ephesians, *Apostolic Fathers*, 86-87.

25 Ignatius, To the Ephesians, *Apostolic Fathers*, 87.

26 Isaiah Berlin, *The Age of Enlightenment: The Eighteenth Century Philosophers* (Cambridge: The Riverside Press, 1956), 113.

27 Berlin, 113.

28 Voltaire, *The Philosophical Dictionary*, selected and translated by H.I. Woolf (New York: Knopf, 1924). The page on "envy" scanned by the Hanover College Department of History in 1995, and found at http://history.hanover.edu/texts/voltaire/volenvy.htm.

Index

This book was designed and set into type
by Mitchell S. Muncy,
with cover design by Lee Whitmarsh,
and printed and bound
by Thomson-Shore, Inc.,
Dexter, Michigan.

The text face is Minion Multiple Master,
designed by Robert Slimbach
and issued in digital form by Adobe Systems,
Mountain View, California, in 1991.

The cover illustration is *The Calling of St. Matthew* by Caravaggio,
Contarelli Chapel, San Luigi dei Francesi, Rome,
reproduced by agreement with Art Resource, New York.

The index is by IndExpert, Fort Worth, Texas.

The paper is acid-free and is of archival quality.

48

52100